The Story of
Yamada Waka

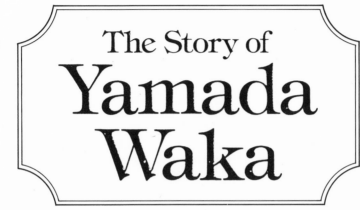

The Story of
Yamada Waka

From Prostitute to Feminist Pioneer

Tomoko Yamazaki

trans. by
Wakako Hironaka & Ann Kostant

KODANSHA INTERNATIONAL
Tokyo, New York & San Francisco

This English edition is adapted with some abridgement from
Ameyuki-san no Uta: Yamada Waka no Sūki Naru Shōgai
published by *Bungei Shunjū*, 1978. All photographs through
the courtesy of *Bungei Shunjū*.
Note: Japanese personal names are given in their usual order,
family name first.

Distributed in the United States by Kodansha Interna-
tional/USA Ltd., through Harper & Row, Publishers, Inc.,
10 East 53rd Street, New York, N.Y. 10022.

Published by Kodansha International Ltd., 12-21 Otowa
2-chome, Bunkyo-ku, Tokyo 112 and Kodansha Interna-
tional/USA Ltd., 10 East 53rd Street, New York, New York
10022 and the Hearst Bldg., 5 Third Street, San Francisco,
California 94103. Copyright in Japan 1985 by Kodansha
International Ltd.
ISBN4-7700-1233-0 (in Japan)
First edition, 1985

Library of Congress Cataloging-in-Publication Data
Yamazaki, Tomoko, 1932–
  The story of Yamada Waka.
  Translation of: Ameyuki-san no Uta: Yamada Waka no
Sūki Naru Shōgai.
  1. Yamada, Waka, 1879–1956. 2. Feminists–Japan–
Biography. I. Title.
HQ1763.Y3913   1985   305.4'2'0924   [B]   85-40042
ISBN 0-87011-733-5

Contents

Yamada Waka and Yamada Kakichi around 1905. This picture
appeared in *Shufunotomo* magazine in October, 1934.

Introduction

$\mathcal{T}$his is a book about a woman named Yamada Waka, an extraordinary woman who lived during a period of rapid social and economic change in Japan. Born into a family whose fortunes declined, she crossed the Pacific Ocean only to meet a worse fate, one not unlike that of hundreds of other Japanese women who came to the West Coast of the United States and Canada around the turn of the century.

Unlike others, Yamada Waka was not easily defeated. Her courage, intelligence and basic honesty helped her to reshape her life and recover from the numerous twists and turns of the early years. When she later returned to Japan, she joined a new elite of men and women. It was the beginning of Taishō Democracy and Waka, together with Yamada Kakichi, who was mentor and friend as well as husband, played a significant role in the circle of intellectuals who were eagerly investigating Western ideas and institutions. Because of their experience in America, their knowledge of English and other factors, the Yamadas were valuable people. Starting out as a translator, Waka herself went on to become a social critic and a nationally known figure.

To better appreciate her story, it is worthwhile to recall the historical background, particularly what Japan was like in the late 19th and early 20th centuries.

In the summer of 1853, a squadron of the US Navy under the command of Commodore Matthew Perry reached Edo Bay and demanded commercial and diplomatic relations between the two countries. It was a case of gunboat diplomacy but it succeeded where the previous importunings of the Western powers had not. Perry's mission not only enticed Japan out of two centuries of self-imposed seclusion but also precipitated one of the most dramatic and far-reaching changes in Japanese history. In the fifteen years after Perry's visit, there was continual factional strife, but in the end the Tokugawa shogunate, governor of the country since 1603, was overthrown. The Meiji Restoration, officially begun in 1868, inaugurated a train of events that made Japan the first non-Western power to promulgate a constitution (1889) and adopt a parliamentary form of government. The new government, under the guise of an emperor ostensibly restored to ancient power and glory, carried out in his name innumerable programs that would transform Japan into a powerful modern nation-state.

In foreign relations, the Meiji government inherited from the old regime a number of unequal treaties between Japan and various Western powers. These treaties placed Japan at a serious disadvantage. For example, Japan was deprived of jurisdiction over aliens on its territory and the right to unilaterally change the 5-percent flat tariff rate. The unequal treaty system hurt Japanese national pride and hampered the economy, but the signatory powers refused to relinquish their privileges until Japan became a "civilized nation." Abolition of the treaty system was, therefore, one of the dominant political issues for several decades.

On the domestic front, spurred by an immense innate curiosity as well as official policy, the Meiji government soon became the prime mover for sweeping changes that affected social, scientific and cultural areas of the nation's life. The opening of Japan's doors to the world set in motion the traffic of goods, ideas and persons from foreign countries, as the government moved to either abolish or modify a number of institutions that had bound together Tokugawa society. A modern banking system, railroads, a telegraph network and an assortment of basic industries, all of which required Western know-how, were created in a matter of years. Both the government and the private sector employed hundreds of men to teach the most advanced industrial and military technology. From English bankers to French jurists to American scientists, engineers and language teachers—from steam engines and gas lamps to parasols and bonnets—Japan was inundated by Western "civilization and enlightenment."

One far-reaching change occurred in the tax system. Formerly, taxes were paid in kind and the farmers, the main taxpayers, annually surrendered up to 40 to 60 percent of the rice harvested from the land they tilled. Under the tax law of 1873, the farmers remained the chief source of revenue, but the tax was levied on the value of farm land and collected in cash from the land owners regardless of the harvest yield. The new tax system, which no doubt weighed heavily on Yamada Waka's family, was a tremendous burden on the small landholder and his meager resources, particularly in the 1880s when deflationary forces aggravated the situation, forcing even middle class farmers into tenantry.

Behind the new tax system were two major financial requirements: the government's priority on creating a strong military and the need to subsidize industrialization in the absence of large-scale private capitalization or foreign loans. For both ventures, the Meiji government required ample and constant revenues.

Industrialization was not the only face of the restoration. Education was a major pillar of government policy, and foreign literature, political and social concepts, arts and sciences filtered rapidly into a society in ferment. At the same time old class distinctions disintegrated. In pursuing its policy of creating a "rich country and a strong military," the government also engendered a certain amount of economic dislocation. The ruling elite of feudal society, the samurai, were replaced by non-hereditary civil administrators and a conscript army. As the samurai class was disbanded, so too were hereditary restrictions removed from the other social and occupational classes of farmer, artisan and merchant. In the end, amid a host of other societal and economic transformations, theoretically at least, social mobility became a fact of national life.

The traffic in goods and people was not one way. In gaining access to Japan's markets, the trading nations also opened up their own markets. And not only were tea and silk exported from Japan, but people also began to go abroad, some for permanent settlement, some to study, and some to be hired as contract or free labor. In one particular group alone, there were about one hundred travelers, not counting retainers and servants.

Only a privileged few journeyed to the West to study and then returned home to fulfilling careers in politics, business, scholarship or art. The vast majority, who went as laborers or emigrants, met a different fate. Those who landed on American or Canadian shores nourished the same hopes and dreams that had brought, and would continue to bring, swarms of Europeans over a period of many decades. Unlike the Europeans for whom America was a haven and a true melting pot, Japanese and other Orientals faced mistreatment, prejudice and cynical exploitation by the more sinister elements of society.

U.S. immigration statistics are unreliable for the early period of Japanese immigration; therefore, to a large extent the Imperial Statistical Annals (Japan) have been used to calculate the number of immigrants. Even so, accurate figures remain elusive. It is known, however, that the whole spectrum of Japanese society was represented: students on government scholarships or privately financed, adventurers of questionable character, seamen who had jumped ship, craftsmen, laborers and so on. Just how many able-bodied men who could neither find work nor return to their homeland eventually wound up as gangsters, gamblers or pimps is not known, but the number who resorted to crime to survive was not insignificant. Women fared still worse; their status was so low that they were not even included in the statistics until around 1900.

Compared to European immigration, which saw 17 million men, women and children crossing the Atlantic between 1880 and 1910, the number of Japanese settling in America was quite small. The figure for 1891 seems to have been around 1 thousand and even in 1900 it was only about 10 thousand.

We should note that despite the colossal changes that overtook Japan, certain qualities in the people remained substantially unaffected by the rush to modernization. One such quality was filial piety; another was the acceptance by women of male authority. After a long feudal past and centuries of Confucian influence, women in Japanese society played an unmistakably subservient role. Under what was in effect a double moral standard, men enjoyed a less restrictive social life and the easy availability of geisha and women of the night. Concubinage and prostitution had long been an integral part of the Japanese social fabric and the latter was not abolished until the mid 1950s. Yoshiwara, Edo's famous licensed quarter, had a history going back three centuries to the building boom that turned the village of Edo into the Tokugawa shoguns' capital.

During the long Meiji period (1868–1912), children still revered parents, wives obeyed husbands, and sisters deferred to brothers. Although families without a male heir might marry off a daughter and then adopt the son-in-law to carry on the family name, for the most part, the continuity of lineage through the male line was the indisputable purpose of life for every member of the family. To the egotism of male lineage, epitomized by paternal authority, the children, and especially the daughters, learned to sacrifice themselves and each other. A family in desperate circumstances might resort to rather cruel treatment of its female members, who were sometimes sold or traded for economic reasons.

Eviscerating the old morality was not an objective of the Meiji Restoration, but it did endeavor to respond to certain demands of the people by creating new institutions in government. Tunes of the new age played side by side with the solemnity of Confucian doctrine. The old morality emphasizing familial obligation continued to prevail in the Meiji state, ensuring peace and stability at home, while experimentation with political freedom (popular representation in the legislature) was carried on, and the House of Japan ruled by the patriarchal emperor was taking its place in the community of nations. Commencing with the restoration of imperial authority in 1868, the work of nation building reached a plateau in 1890 when the newly created National Diet began to deliberate affairs of state. Internationally, the "strong country" policy showed evidence of success as Japan won a war against China (1895) and further confounded the international community ten years later by winning a second war against Russia.

The history of Japan between Perry's visit and the Sino-Japanese War illuminates two major events in the life of Yamada Waka: her marriage and her decision to go to America. She was born in 1879 into a farming family whose fortunes were declining just as she was reaching marriageable age. Although impossible to document, it seems very likely that the decline in the family's fortunes coincided with the nationwide rise of tenantry attributable to the Land Tax Reform Law of 1873 and the government's instigation of stringent, recessionary fiscal policies in the early 1880s. For a family facing hard times, a daughter like Waka, that is, not only marriageable but, as the fifth of eight children, expendable, was a natural way out of a tight situation. In the light of the age-old virtue of filial piety instilled both in the family and the schools, a girl in Waka's position had no grounds for resistance, regardless of the personal consequences such a marriage might bring.

In a way, her decision to go to America also reflected history. Kanagawa Prefecture, where she was born, had one of the seven ports opened to foreign ships and traders under the new treaties. Yokohama was close to Tokyo, and in no time it became the busiest and most prosperous of the treaty ports. Foreign diplomats en route to the capital disembarked there, as did a good number of traders; before long there were English signboards framing Japanese buildings. This area bordering the west side of Tokyo Bay became one of the industrial centers of Japan with the emphasis on ship building. In short, Yamada Waka's hometown was only a stone's throw from Japan's gate to the outside world. By electing to go abroad when women from other parts of Japan in need of work made their way to textile mills, Yamada, in a sense, seized an opportunity that the port town offered. It was a fateful step in an extraordinary life.

As noted previously, Japanese immigrants in America had a history of unexpected disappointments. Their patience and hard work, often meagerly compensated, were necessarily pitted against covert and overt racial prejudice. By the 1880s, when Asian immigrants began to arrive, the West Coast had already been declared white man's territory for at least half a century. Although the earliest official discrimination was leveled specifically against the first to arrive, the Chinese (Chinese Exclusion Act of 1882), there was always a possibility of legally sanctioned discrimination against the Japanese. This became a reality in the so-called Gentlemen's Agreement of 1907, according to which entry of Japanese common laborers into the United States was expressly forbidden.

Even when they landed on American soil legally, Japanese and other Asians experienced discrimination in a number of forms: backbreaking jobs in railroad construction or mining paid barely a subsistence wage, as did the farm work or menial jobs white people relinquished because they no longer wanted them. Newcomers without scruples and those for whom survival was a matter of desperation resorted to racketeering and gambling.

Aggravating matters was the tremendous sexual imbalance. At least until 1909, Japanese men greatly outnumbered Japanese women (in 1900 by as much as twenty-four to one), and they could not marry Caucasoid women. Prostitution was an obvious outlet. Or as portrayed by Kafu Nagai in *Amerika Monogatari* ("American Tales"), incidents were reported of Japanese living in places far from brothels gang-raping the wives of other men. Clearly, for a great number the dream of sending money to families back in Japan turned out to be virtually impossible. It was difficult enough to earn enough to stay alive.

For women, life was measurably more difficult. In the first place, women of the lower classes were not issued passports, this being one reason why statistics on the number of women immigrants are unreliable or non-existent. Most disembarked into a world of extreme hardship; whether they boarded ship in Yokohama of their own volition or were white slaved by pimps or procuresses was of no consequence. Once on board, the young women were cruelly treated and sometimes abused during the voyage itself. Quite a few did not survive the crossing. Lacking passports, many who did survive had to be smuggled into the country. In some instances, women were packed into wooden boxes and carted ashore as cargo; others were tossed over the side of the ship to swim ashore—or drown.

Vancouver, British Columbia, figured as an important port of landing because Canadian immigration officials were less rigid than those south of the border. From Vancouver, girls were transported to the Yukon or to Seattle, Portland or San Francisco. Whatever the direction it meant going straight into the dreadful humiliation of brothel life.

In the late 1890s the brothels around Seattle's King Street showed an increase in numbers. One Japanese official, Fujita Yoshiro, made an inspection trip of the Pacific Northwest in July, 1891, to determine the circumstances of the Japanese living in that area. He reported that:

In Seattle, there is one grocery store and ten restaurants owned and operated by Japanese, and approximately 250 Japanese live there at present. Of these 250, only 40 have steady jobs as proprietors and employees of the grocery and restaurants. Another 200, if not prostitutes or owners of houses of pleasure, are either gamblers or pimps. Some of the restaurants themselves are operated in conjunction with a house of pleasure, either separately or as part of a single establishment. In short, five or six of the restaurants are connected in one way or another with prostitution. In the city of Seattle, I can discern only 10 individuals who have absolutely nothing to do with either prostitution or gambling and who are, in the strict sense, engaged in a legitimate business or occupation.

Fujita found similar conditions in Spokane, Washington, where he observed that out of sixty Japanese in the city, forty-seven were pimps, prostitutes or gamblers.

There is considerable documentation on prostitution in Seattle at that time. An interesting account is given by Itō Kazuo in his book, *One Hundred Years of Cherry Trees in North America*. He confirms that Oriental women of pleasure were separated into two categories—those reserved for whites and those for non-whites. By 1902 there were some 200 prostitutes in Seattle.

A similar demimonde existed in Portland, Oregon. With regard to this, Fujita comments:

Most Japanese men I saw there tried to avoid meeting or having a conversation with me. Then I learned that most of the women had come from Seattle, having been brought from there by Japanese sailors who had jumped ship. These sailors, either as a prostitute's husband or her employer, have forced many Japanese women to practice prostitution. At present, there are about forty of these pimps in the city. . . . To my surprise I found two or three former students among the pimps. I was told they had given up their studies in San Francisco and drifted to this city.

On my way back to San Francisco by train, I made in-

quiries at every stop concerning the presence of Japanese.
As a result of these inquiries I have learned that there is
a group of Japanese in almost all of those places along the
way. They were, however, either prostitutes or their
employers; none were engaged in legitimate businesses or
occupations.

A more elite class of women also came to America, but
only after the confirmation of Hawaii as an American territory in 1900. (Emigration to Hawaii, the first from Japan
to the U.S., had begun fifteen years earlier.) The voyage for
some was arranged as part of the picture-bride custom, a few
came as students, and others were wives of officials. On the
East Coast, it should be noted, lower class women found
employment as maids for upper class families.

For young women like Yamada Waka, who had at most
only a letter of introduction to a stranger in a strange land,
there was bound to be hardship. Probably for the majority
life never became any better. Yamada was fortunate in this
respect, and when she and her husband returned to Japan,
the country was on the eve of a major historical development. By her victories against China and Russia, Japan not
only rid herself of unequal treaties but also acquired overseas
territories.

The country was now fully caught up in the industrial
revolution, and the increase of the proletarian class and
landless farmers heightened egalitarian aspirations, as attested
to by the founding of the Japan Socialist Party in 1906. The
National Diet was well into its second decade and political
parties were growing more impatient with the practice of

"transcendental cabinets," whereby the emperor appointed prime ministers who lacked party support. Legal scholars, such as Minobe Tatsukichi, and writers like those of the Shirakaba school, expressed hope for a more liberal and democratic society. It was the beginning of the spirit of individualism, the dawn of Taishō Democracy.

Taishō Democracy actually began a few years before 1912, the year the Meiji Emperor died and was seceded by his son, who took the reign name Taishō. The Taishō Emperor's health prevented him from being a man like his father was. Nevertheless, the democratic movement thrived through the years of World War I and the Russian Revolution, awakening along the way women and workers to their entitlement to the rights of representation. Two milestones were passed when the majority party headed by Hara Kei formed a government (1918) and the Universal Manhood Suffrage Movement succeeded in extending the franchise from tax-paying men to all men in 1925.

To the extent that the new suffrage law did not give women voting rights, Taishō Democracy proved to be a male political movement. It was, however, not without significance for feminism in Japan. In it, through it, women confidently voiced their desire for more individual and political freedom and equal opportunity with men.

One small but significant organization in the development of Japanese feminism was the Seitōsha ("Bluestocking Society," 1911–16). With its appearance, women perhaps reached a turning point. Seitōsha members showed a definite trend from a belief in purely personal solutions to women's frustrations to a concern with the entire structure of their society, and, finally, to the advocacy of various actions that would change the social structure. Contributors to the movement's magazine, *Seitō*, dealt with women's problems in marriage and society as a whole and, indeed, represented the spirit of the new women.

A key figure was Hiratsuka Raichō. Perhaps even more than Yamada Waka, she embodied Taishō Democracy as it applied to women. Born and raised in Tokyo, Hiratsuka attended an upper middle class girl's academy and then went on to a women's college. She did a great deal of soul-searching at an early age, became interested in Zen Buddhism, met other intellectuals, formed the Seitōsha and later, with Ichikawa Fusae, established the New Woman's Association. It was Hiratsuka's unique emphasis on personal freedom that in some sense makes her the true child of the Taishō period.

She was truly a remarkable person—flamboyant, creative, given to experimenting with life styles and courageous. She and Yamada, despite close personal ties, diverged widely on political and social issues. Hiratsuka accented personal freedom while Yamada, in the final analysis, moved towards more traditional values: emperor, family and state.

Seitōsha was essentially a literary group. In the first issue of its journal. Hiratsuka penned a manifesto that has become famous:

> In the beginning, woman was the sun,
> A true person.
> Now she is the moon—pale as if ill,
> Aglow but in the light of another.

Arise, woman, retrieve the sun,
Your hidden sun.
Pray, manifest your hidden sun,
Your long-buried genius!

Hiratsuka's faith in women's creative powers appealed to many souls who sought self-realization. Among the receptive ones were a number who have earned a lasting place in modern Japanese history: the poetess Yosano Akiko; writer and literary critic Nogami Yaeko; journalist and postwar Diet member Ichikawa Fusae; and Yamada Waka herself. Waka's husband Kakichi found Hiratsuka's feminism too individualistic and did not encourage his wife to join Hiratsuka in the New Woman's Association. Founded in 1920, the group offered several rallying points for women from all walks of life. Its focal interest was on female suffrage. Instead of joining, Waka chose to publish her own journal, *Fujin to Shinshakai* ("Women and the New Society"). Still, the fact remains that through Seitōsha, Waka earned a reputation as a translator and social critic. She too, it seems, was a child of Taishō Democracy.

No doubt it is trite to say that the history of a nation like the life of an individual has many twists and turns. Yet risking banality is warranted by both Japanese history and Yamada's life after the Taishō Emperor's death in 1926. Following a twenty-year interlude of political and personal freedom and intermittent economic booms, the Japanese began in the late 1920s to descend steadily into a dark valley characterized by political suppression at home and military aggression abroad. The communist and other working class

movements that showed unexpected strength in the first national election under the new law were ruined by the arrest,
assassination or recantation of their leaders and followers.
The collapse of the New York stock market in 1929 depressed
the Japanese economy too. Economic blocs, built to protect
the colonial powers of the West, deprived Japan of overseas
markets. Poor harvests caused by cold summers further
burdened the weakened economy. Parents in dire financial
straits resorted to the old solution of selling daughters to
brothels, while sons went into the army. The political parties offered no quick remedy. Through adroit maneuvering,
the military took over the government. The Diet became a
rubber stamp. Then as strategic considerations necessitated
total mobilization, the family-state ideology was invoked to
buttress the military effort. The cardinal virtues of loyalty
and filial piety were sacrosanct, and women were encouraged
to, "*Umeyō, fuyaseyō,*" literally, "Reproduce, multiply."

Against this background, Yamada Waka catapulted into
national fame by accepting the nomination to the chairman-
ship of the Motherhood Protection League. Other luminous
assignments followed, casting her in the role of the ideal
Japanese woman and mother. These developments were
perhaps natural for Yamada, who had clasped Hiratsuka's
newborn baby to her bosom like a treasure and carried it
from the hospital to the mother's home. Hiratsuka, whose
father donned a frockcoat to visit the Meiji Emperor in the
palace and gave his daughter all the privileges and protection a family such as his could afford, became an ardent advocate of women's freedom from conventional familial stric-
tures, especially female servitude in marriage to preserve the

male lineage. Yamada, on the other hand, who sacrificed herself to save her parental farming household, blossomed as a supporter of family and motherhood. Her glory was perhaps also the tragedy of the prewar Japanese family and social system.

The Japanese military government of the thirties, of course, valued Waka's ideas and used her for propaganda purposes. Nevertheless, in 1937 Eleanor Roosevelt did receive Yamada Waka at the White House, which clearly indicates that in the United States at least she was not really associated with militaristic notions. After the war, she was all but forgotten, possibly because she had allowed herself to be so used.

In the pages that follow, the reader will see how the author has picked up the threads of this remarkable story and woven them into an inspiring tapestry. It was not an easy task. So many years had passed, so many memories faded, and in a number of cases people were reluctant to part with information, or would do so only when anonymity was assured. (In this adaptation, certain names have been changed out of consideration for the individuals concerned.) We are deeply indebted to her for her perseverance. And we, the translators, are also greatly indebted to Akiko Hirai for her invaluable research and assistance in helping us prepare this introduction.

Prologue

$\mathcal{W}$ell do I recall that dazzling sunset. From the plane's small window I watched the fiery ball descend below the horizon as thousands of sharp golden arrows flashed across the sky and gradually softened into a purple-shaped umbrella. What a spectacle!

I remember, too, being affected by more than the visual. Ordinarily, the sight of the fading sun would have made me feel terribly anxious. Often, while observing the onset of evening or clouds turning red over the western mountains, I experience a strange malaise that has been with me since childhood. I immediately long for home and the comforts of family life. But there I was, bound for Tokyo, and rather wishing I had stayed in San Francisco, since there were two very old people whom I desperately wanted to interview and I had a presentiment that time was running out.

It had all begun two weeks earlier, on October 18, 1975, the day I left Japan to make a lecture tour of the United States at the invitation of an airline company and a travel agency.

After a ten-hour flight, I arrived at San Francisco International Airport, and tired as I was, I'll never forget my first impression of the West Coast. The highway and buildings from the airport to the city were unremarkable, but once in the city proper, I had to tell myself more than once that I was no longer home. The lay of the city reminded me of Nagasaki, with its narrow streets winding around the hills. Still, San Francisco had its wide avenues, trees and modern buildings, neatly arranged, and I did not encounter crowds like those in Tokyo or Nagasaki.

I checked into the Miyako Hotel, rested a bit, and then went on to a party at a nearby Japanese restaurant. About a hundred others had been invited, a mix of Japanese businessmen and counselor corps, and second and third generation Japanese-Americans. Cocktails preceded dinner.

I chose to sit next to a middle-aged woman who said she owned a local bar. Our conversation was soon interrupted by an older man seated across from us. When he finally caught my attention, he inquired whether I had ever heard of Yamada Waka. From the wrinkles and the white beard covering half his face I guessed he was in his late sixties, but the sparkle in his eyes had an attractive youthfulness.

"Yamada Waka? Of course," I replied. "She was a well-known feminist author during the twenties and thirties, but forgotten by now. Her husband was the scholar Yamada Kakichi. I happen to have read four or five of her works because I'm interested in the women's movement."

He gulped down the last of his drink, leaned forward, and looked alternately at the bar owner and me. "There are very few people now who remember that Yamada Waka spent several years in this country serving white males. Yes, yes. She was one of those women. She was known as 'The Arabian Oyae.' Yamazaki-san, I read your book *Sandakan*. Saw the movie, too. Do you know that similar stories could be written about a lot of other Japanese women who came to the West Coast? Yamada Waka, for instance?"

I was stunned. I nearly dropped my glass. When I got back to the hotel, I flopped into bed, dead tired after many hours of travel and an exhausting evening. I tossed and turned, took a sleeping pill and watched the stars, but my thoughts kept drifting back to Yamada.

I thought of a short passage from Hiratsuka Raichō's *Autobiography*. Hiratsuka was the founder and prime mover behind the Japanese women's movement. At the time of her death in 1971 she was eighty-five. When I met her in her declining years, she was confined to her bed, from which she wrote and revised her autobiography. It was published posthumously in four volumes.

In one chapter, which she called "The Strange Fortunes of Yamada Waka's Early Years," she described how she met Yamada Kakichi and Waka when she had been the editor of the woman's magazine *Seitō* ("Bluestocking"). I remember having especially questioned the authenticity of the following information:

Waka came from a poor peasant family living near Misaki, Kanagawa Prefecture. When she could no longer bear to watch her parents toil night and day in the fields to provide for their large family, she decided to go to America and earn enough to send money home. But on the West

Coast she discovered that hard work alone was not suffi-
cient and soon wound up in a brothel. Yamada Kakichi,
whom I'd been told was once badly injured while working
on a ranch, had been pursuing his studies when one day
he happened to meet Waka on the street. Attracted by
her innate goodness and natural beauty, he decided to save
her from her unfortunate situation.

The passage had been hard to swallow. Not that I doubted
Hiratsuka's integrity; a person of her stature was not likely
to fabricate such a story. Besides, she had pointed out in a
footnote that the source of her information had been Yamada
herself; the two had been close friends.

Despite Hiratsuka's assurances I had remained skeptical.
Was it conceivable that one of society's elite, known to
millions as a columnist, author, critic and translator, had been
an ordinary prostitute? And if so, how did she manage to
escape the stigma of her past? I inferred that Yamada's whole
life, not just those "early years" as Hiratsuka thought, had
been full of "strange incidents." How else could an outcast
from society "have climbed to a place in the sun?" From my
familiarity with prostitutes I knew it had to have been an
uphill battle.

After my encounter with the old man in San Francisco,
I began to think that Hiratsuka's comment on Waka contained more fact than fiction. "How truly incredible," I said
to myself over and over, unable to dismiss the haunting image of the young Yamada.

My thoughts eventually drifted to my own works on such
women. In the first, *Sandakan No. 8 Brothel*, the heroine Saki

leads the typical life of a streetwalker after she is sent abroad by Japanese white slavers. Her story was based on real events in the life of a certain *Karayuki-san*. The Saki in real life is shriveled up, hopelessly impoverished and adopts a pragmatic philosophy of resignation that enables her to go on living. With many years of debauchery behind her, a mature, resigned Saki becomes an expert at surviving.

Hirata Yuki and Ogawa Fumi in *The Tomb of Sandakan* are also compelled to sell themselves. Both despise their situation, all the more so because they are in a foreign country and cannot converse with their clients. Somehow they manage to escape and start over; but it does not work out. Yuki commits suicide and Fumi disappears, no one knows where.

Neither Yuki nor Fumi is able to set herself free despite a strong will and the determination to do so. Their past acts like an iron chain. Common sense dictates that their position is futile. Indeed, if the burden of the past becomes unbearable, as it did in Yuki's case, suicide may appear as a reasonable alternative. Most women simply return to their former ways. In any event, all the Karayuki-san I have known are losers. Another writer on the subject, Morisaki Kazue, agrees with me. One of the characters in her book *Karayuki-san* goes insane and the other takes her own life.

I suppose that a prostitute who is beautiful, sexually exciting or talented has a chance of becoming a high class mistress, the wife of a rich man, or even a famous personality, Edith Piaff or Billie Halliday style. But Yamada Waka's accomplishments demanded good judgment, intelligence and a fair amount of scholarly knowledge. To have become one

of the leading figures of her time, she must have undergone
several continuous transformations that, in turn, must have
invited all sorts of "strange incidents." At least that is what
I conjectured.

Light streamed in and I still could not sleep. The strange
coincidence that I, author of two books on Karayuki-san,
had landed in America and had immediately heard of another
such case, led me to believe—although I am not at all
superstitious—that I was being guided by a mysterious thread
of destiny. My whole being at that moment felt the resent-
ment and wounds of the many young Japanese women who
had crossed the Pacific only to end up selling their bodies.
I resolved to console their spirits by writing Yamada Waka's
biography. It would be called "The Life of an Ameyuki-san."
I hoped that many unfortunates would become inspired and
recognize that will, determination and intelligence can exert
an influence on, if not totally change, an otherwise hopeless
destiny. [*Ame* is an abbreviated word for America. *Kara*
specifically means China, but in a broader sense includes the
rest of East and Southeast Asia. The meaning of *yuki* is "going." Eventually, these two colloquial expressions, *Karayuki-
san* and *Ameyuki-san*, came to refer to women who went
abroad and were sexually exploited.]

At the time I decided to look into Waka's life, I knew very
little about her, but of course, I was eager to learn more.
Before beginning my lecture tour, I decided to speak to the
man I had met the night before at the reception. Shimizu
Iwao was president of the *Hokubei Mainichi Shimbun*, a
Japanese newspaper long published in San Francisco.

"I expected you to contact me," he said with a friendly

twinkle. "You want to investigate Yamada Waka's past, don't you?" As he talked, he nodded his head affirmatively, implying that my efforts would be rewarded.

"Yes," I admitted. Then I asked if there was anyone still alive who might have known Yamada in her youth.

He said that all his information about Yamada had come to him secondhand. After taking a moment to think it over, he suggested I get in touch with a certain Kitano Motoji, a man of ninety, who used to own a Chinatown hotel in the midst of the brothels. "He may have known her," said Shimizu. "Another possibility is Izumi Ie. She owned the Otafuku Tei restaurant. She must be about ninety-four now, but I believe she used to know every Japanese person in town."

I would have liked to visit the two of them right then and there, but my schedule was tight. Besides, I knew from past experience that when planning to interview old people, it was better not to be impatient. Also, if I waited a little, it would give me the opportunity to do some research beforehand.

"I'm sorry, Shimizu-san. I can't take the time right now. But I have every intention of coming back to see them and I hope you'll introduce me to them at that time."

For the next two weeks I lectured all over the country and then returned to San Francisco. When I left for Japan, I had the feeling, as I watched the sky turn bright red and orange, that I ought to have stayed in America, at least long enough to meet the two possible witnesses from Yamada Waka's youth.

Ichikawa Fusae

$\mathcal{B}$ack home I counted the days until I could listen to the stories of the old man and woman in San Francisco. Sometimes even in the midst of other assignments (quite a bit had piled up during my absence) the blazing sunset intruded in a mystical way into my thoughts.

I set aside a few hours each day to collect Yamada's books and articles, a task that proved to be more difficult than I could have anticipated. I personally possessed five of her works, including her revealing essays on the subject of "Love in our Society."

I began my hunt methodically. I covered every used book store in Jimbōchō, a district in central Tokyo famous for old, rare or simply hard-to-find publications and prints. But there was nothing, and in the libraries, Yamada's name was rarely on file, nor had librarians heard of her. And this was a woman who had been a prominent contributor to *Seitō* and a popular columnist for the *Tokyo Asahi*, a newspaper for which she wrote an Ann Landers type column. So quickly forgotten? I was dismayed. Out of sight, out of mind. The cliche certainly applied in this case.

Eventually, persistence paid off. I gradually added to my collection quite a number of her books and articles, each of which I perused as quickly as water filters through sand. But I learned very little from them about Yamada Waka herself. Her fiction seemed to lack specific, or even subtle, indirect references to her own life. Here and there, I did come across phrases that intimated a life of misery. In one place I read, "Stumbling about in the hopeless darkness, stained with blood, I was merely surviving." In another, "Since I had seen families fall into misery because of the loose conduct of men, those women who play the coquette for money with men whose only motive is material and carnal desire are . . ." Still, the writing was so abstract, I could hardly reconstruct Yamada's early life from such fragments.

Yamada was born in 1879 and most of her contemporaries were gone, but two of them, Yamataka Shigeri and Ichikawa Fusae, were still alive. I wrote to the latter first, since she was likely to know more about Yamada. Together with Hiratsuka Raichō, Ichikawa had established the New Women's Association. Now eighty-two and having been elected four times, she carried on her efforts on behalf of women in the House of Councillors of the National Diet.

I wondered whether she would spare the time to see me, and if she did, whether she would be inclined to discuss Waka. I had high hopes that she could tell me how Yamada had found her way to America.

She agreed to talk to me, and on a bitterly cold day in November I went to her office. I was met by a lovely, silver-

Ichikawa Fusae (1893–1981), in the forefront of women's causes for many decades, was elected to the House of Councillors five times in the post-war years.

haired woman, slim and graceful, who greeted me in a very friendly fashion, as if we had known one another for many years.

"So, you've come at last, Yamazaki-san," she said. "Believe it or not, I've been expecting you since your *Sandakan* series was published."

Without further ado she plunged into the past. Skipping about in time, she blended and interwove stories about Yamada and others with tales from her own life. She talked on at length and ended up running well over the alloted time. In essence, the following is what she told me.

"I met Waka in Tokyo in the summer of 1918. I was twenty-five and had recently arrived in the big city from Aichi Prefecture where I was born and raised. I had three brothers and three sisters. My youth can be summed up in a nutshell. I grew up in Nishio City, attended Aichi Women's Normal School—because tuition was free—graduated, and became an elementary school teacher." She also became the first woman journalist for the *Nagoya Shimbun* but, she said, "I was still not satisfied with what a woman's life had to offer. I dreamed of going to Tokyo, of meeting new faces and learning new ideas."

An opportunity finally presented itself in the summer of 1918 when a friend left for Tokyo and some months later encouraged Ichikawa to join her. She immediately wrote to her eldest brother Fujichi, who was then a journalist in San Francisco. In his reply, her brother urged her to call on a certain Yamada Kakichi, who, he said, was "a fine, sincere man." He noted that Yamada had taught him English when he first arrived in San Francisco in the early 1900s.

By taking her brother's advice Ichikawa met Yamada Waka, who did not strike her as a career woman when they were first introduced. At that time the Yamadas depended entirely on Kakichi's income from private language lessons. He had a lot of students because of his reputation for fluency in French, English, Spanish and German. Hiratsuka Raichō was one of his followers. Another was the famous anarchist Ōsugi Sakae. He was assassinated in Tokyo by military police during the turmoil after the terrible earthquake and fire of 1923. His wife Itō Noe and their child were also killed along with him.

"You know, Yamazaki-san, that Itō Noe had been the editor in chief of *Seitō*," she reminisced. "I was still at the Aichi Normal School when I read about the contributors to that magazine, women who were openly criticized for drinking exotic wines and liquors. Later on, in Nagoya, I happened to buy a copy of *Seitō*, which did not impress me at all. I noticed Itō's name on the masthead, but I don't remember seeing Yamada's, although she was an important writer and translator of articles for it. In fact, it wasn't until I visited the Yamadas that I discovered that Waka was anything other than an ordinary housewife."

Ichikawa said that Kakichi had barely completed the third grade when he was sent away from home to become an apprentice of some sort. He was eight. Later he got to America, worked at manual jobs—dishwasher here, ranch hand there—and saved his money to buy books, from which he taught himself all those languages. He had been quite a remarkable person, she thought.

"I'd like to tell you just what happened on my first visit because it had a tremendous impact on my future. From the beginning Kakichi and Waka seemed interested in my welfare. They found a small room for me on the second floor of a house of a charcoal dealer in their neighborhood. But even at four yen a month the room was too expensive for me. Eager as I was to come in contact with new ideas, I needed a job. The Yamadas helped me with everything.

"When I decided it would be useful to learn English so I could read foreign literature, Kakichi began to teach me for half an hour before work every morning. I went to my first lesson with only a smattering of English from my Aichi school days. I was stupefied by Kakichi's choice of text: Ellen Kay's *Love and Marriage*, translated from the Swedish."

Not long afterwards Ichikawa was introduced to Hiratsuka Raichō, who, contrary to every rumor circulating about her, was small, beautiful and soft-spoken. They got to know one another pretty quickly and then formed the New Women's Association. That was in March, 1920. Since that time Ichikawa had consecrated her life to women's causes.

She remembered Waka as being quite plain, darker skinned than the average Japanese woman and heavy set: big in every way like a working man. But the sparkle in her eyes, her charm and a fetching motherliness more than compensated for her physical appearance. Strangers and guest alike appreciated her warmth and hospitality. When an outsider happened to be in the Yamada house at dinner time, Waka insisted he or she stay for the meal, however simple. The food on the table was never anything special. The Yamadas were not accustomed to extravagance.

Waka was seven or eight years older than Hiratsuka and exactly fourteen years older than Ishikawa. "Raichō and I used to call her 'Owaka-san,'" she recalled. Such a form of address would be used between equals or when talking to a servant. "We addressed her husband as 'Kakichi-sensei' or 'Yamada-sensei,'" that is, much more formally, as one might speak to a doctor or professor. "Somehow her familiar, embracing, generous personality invited the affectionate form. But you would have had to know her to understand what I mean."

Waka had not been educated past the fourth grade. Whatever else she learned came from Kakichi, her mentor,

Hiratsuka Raichō at the age of thirty-seven (1923). At the time, she was one of the leaders of the New Women's Association.

twelve years her senior, and a kind of father to her. Ironically, in his advanced years, Waka cared for him with a lover's tenderness. Before that it had been Kakichi who worried over and mothered his spouse. In fact, he was so protective that Waka was not permitted to travel outside of Tokyo.

In the summer of 1919 the *Nagoya Shimbun* asked Ichikawa to arrange to have Yamada and Hiratsuka address a summer seminar they were sponsoring for women. Kakichi refused to let his wife go unless Ichikawa promised to accompany her. When the three of them reached the inn in Nagoya, Waka immediately sent off a telegram saying, "Arrived safely, don't worry."

It was their first lecture. Yamada had written down her entire speech beforehand and practically read it to the audience, while Hiratsuka, it seems, did the same, but her voice carried so poorly that she could scarcely be heard. Frequent lecturing eventually altered their style. Yamada even came to be considered a good speaker.

Ichikawa said that all she knew about Waka's unfortunate experience in America came from Hiratsuka, in whom Waka had confided on the night after the Nagoya lectures. When the seminar was over, Hiratsuka was curious to observe women's working conditions in a nearby spinning mill in Okazaki. Since it was near her home, Ichikawa took them there and had them lodged for the night at a small inn, a charming place surrounded by primroses and overlooking the lovely Yahagi River. It must have been there, after she left them to visit her family, that Waka revealed her secret to her friend. She tried to make sure the story would not spread.

"I don't mind, but Daddy would be upset. So please don't tell anyone," Waka implored. By "Daddy" she meant Kakichi.

According to Ichikawa that was why very few people knew about it directly from Yamada herself. "Though the details are sketchy," she told me, "From what I could gather Waka had once been kept in a brothel somewhere in America—a life she despised. Always surrounded by guards, she had to fashion a rope out of bedsheets and climb down from a second or third story window. Kakichi must have told her how to do it. A real romantic thriller, don't you agree?"

Ichikawa's account of Yamada's escape seemed well within the realm of probability. Around 1920 there had been similar tales concerning Salvation Army activities in Yoshiwara, an old and notorious redlight district in Tokyo. People had been beaten up by gangsters employed by pimps—nearly murdered in risking their lives to help prostitutes.

Ichikawa was under the impression that it was Kakichi who had set Waka free, then married her, brought her back to Japan, and taught her everything he knew. She felt that a woman who had become accustomed to selling herself would find it difficult to return to a normal life, but Waka must have been an exception. She had enormous respect for Waka, but added that "Kakichi should be admired even more."

It was a moving and incredible tale I heard that day. I agreed with Ichikawa that many men might be generous and sympathetic to a woman in Waka's situation, perhaps help her in some way, but I could not think of anyone who would marry her. Kakichi was indeed a rarity, an extraordinary man of courage. I was deeply impressed by his desire to broaden Waka's intellectual capabilities. Men often prefer a non-intellectual, hence subservient, companion; Kakichi was different. If more men followed his example women would have far less to complain about. I am in my forties and have witnessed many a bright, clever young girl enter matrimony only to lose her ability to think because she is constantly beset by household duties.

And what an ingenious, dramatic escape Kakichi had devised! Whether he actually took part or just instructed Waka was not clear. In any event, the undertaking was dangerous and he must surely have risked his life. There must have been a pimp involved who would have searched in desperation for the escapee, since she represented a precious source of income to him. Only passion and love could have driven Kakichi to take such a chance, although Waka no doubt emanated a certain purity, like the lotus blooming in a muddy swamp.

I was disappointed that Ichikawa Fusae had not been able to tell me about Waka's family, her upbringing or how she got to America. She did mention in passing that Waka was born on the Miura Peninsula in Kanagawa Prefecture and suggested that I contact Waka's grandson Kunihisa for more information about Waka's early years.

Ichikawa said that Waka, like many women who have suffered the same fate, had lost the ability to conceive. Because of this, she and Kakichi arranged a match between Kakichi's nephew and Waka's niece and then adopted the couple as their children. There was nothing unusual in this. Adoption has long been a traditional method of preserving the family name.

The child of that match is a man named Kunihisa. Until recently he was headmaster of the Hatagaya Girl's School, once a rehabilitation center for wayward girls founded by Yamada Waka. Ichikawa thought Kunihisa would understand my motives for trying to recapture Waka's past.

Along with a letter addressed to him at the Hatagaya Girl's School in which I explained my intentions, I sent Kunihisa my two previous books on prostitutes. He did not respond. With some reluctance I again turned to Ichikawa, who got in touch with him and set up a meeting in her office. There I repeated my plea for his help and collaboration. His expression was stoic.

"Yamada Waka was our grandmother and we cherish her memory," he finally said quietly. "My wife and I have two daughters, one in high school, one in junior high. I don't want to disturb their image of their great-grandmother."

His reaction was natural for one with daughters of a sensitive age. No one in his position would be at all eager to acknowledge that a close relative had once been in a brothel. Yet, while I thoroughly comprehended his desire to protect his children and his family name, I believed he should have been able to place social considerations above family reputation. Waka could inspire hope in women of misfortune who need a model to summon up their courage to change their destiny. It was with this sense of obligation towards such women that I felt compelled to pursue Yamada's life. I argued with Kunihisa that he ought to feel a similar sense of responsibility towards the girls at the rehabilitation center. As for his daughters, I thought that they, along with their peers, should know that many years ago some poor young girls had been sold and forced into prostitution so that their families could survive.

I pleaded with him but no matter what I said he would not change his mind.

Several days after that encounter I became very depressed. Sometimes when I closed my eyes I imagined the purplish red sky above San Francisco. More than ever I wanted to cross the ocean but I knew that I had to investigate Yamada's childhood first, despite the seemingly dead end.

A
Sixteen-year-old
Bride

*T*hinking of the wasted lives of
the prostitutes I had met over the years acted as an incen-
tive to overcome obstacles, including personal disappointments. For the next several days I carefully reexamined
Yamada's writings in search of clues to her childhood. Then
I decided to make the short trip to her native village on the
Miura Peninsula.

In my conversation with Kunihisa I had learned that
Waka's maiden name was Asaba and that she was born in
Kurihama, a district now within the city of Yokosuka, Japan's
first naval base dating back just a century. There is an
American naval base there now. Beyond its reputation for
the vices that plague any military installation, I had no idea
what the city was like.

I left for Yokosuka early one morning. Situated at the
mouth of Tokyo Bay, it is no great distance from Tokyo, but
the train stopped so often that the trip took more than an
hour.

Americans in Japan

Yokosuka's streets are lined with shops, and the billboards and signs above restaurants and clothing stores are mainly in English, no doubt to attract American sailors. None were around then since it was still early in the day. I imagined that towards evening they would file into the bars and cabarets where plenty of women would be waiting to cater to them. I could not help thinking that Yokosuka, sitting there on the west side of the Pacific Ocean, was somehow a fitting location for an Ameyuki-san. At the entrance to Kurihama harbor I paused over the historic inscription: "Commodore Perry's Landing 1853."

At Yokosuka City Hall the clerk went through the records and came back to me with the Asabas' address: 13 Kurihama 1-chome. There it was! My heart pounded with excitement. I set off in the direction of the residential section of Kurihama, which at the time the Asabas had lived there was called Kumura. Numerous small houses intruded into what I imagined was once a peaceful landscape of gentle hills and winding streams. Then again, compared with Tokyo, Kumura's houses were rather large with nice gardens and trees. Throughout the country cities impinge on the surrounding communities for living space, and I suspected that the Miura Peninsula was too close to Tokyo and Yokohama to have been spared.

For the next couple of hours I wandered through Kumura, passing all the sacred landmarks—the Hachiman Shrine among tiny inlets, the Segyōji temple, the tomb of Samura Shinzaemon, a venerated villager who had dammed the Hirasaku River to increase the acreage of the rice fields, and the Mitaki Shrine atop a steep hill where I sat down to rest.

Soon an old man, casually attired in a short jacket, came trudging up the hillside pushing his bike. He was out of breath as he squatted down near me.

"Excuse me," I said, "do you live around here?"

"Yes, my family's been here for generations. Why?" His curiosity became even keener when I explained who I wanted to find out about.

"Yamada Waka." He enunciated the name slowly, with respect. "Nowadays hardly anyone asks about her. I doubt any of the young people have ever heard of her."

He hesitated before continuing. "So you're from Tokyo, eh? This place is not like it used to be. One by one my friends have died. There's practically no one left to talk to about the good old days. Our children grow up and go off to earn big wages in the big cities. Sometimes there aren't enough hands to help in the fields. Here I am . . . in my middle seventies . . . but I vividly remember how it was in Kumura when I was growing up."

Kumura, it seemed, was a name derived from Kurihama and had been the village section of Kurihama. Many thousands of years ago the whole area had been under the sea. Construction workers were always digging into layers of sand mixed with sea shells.

"About Yamada-san, now . . ." he paused again. "To my knowledge there were no Asabas on the Miura Peninsula other than those in Kumura. Their house was over there, close to the beach, right in front of the Hachiman Shrine. People called it Mori no Ie because of the dense forest in back. It's hard now to visualize what it was like, but it must have appeared substantial standing there amidst all those trees.

"I was told that the Asabas had been well off once, maybe the wealthiest household in the village. They had owned field after field, those mountains too. But that was before my time. According to my grandfather, the Asabas used to hire extra help during the planting and harvesting of their rice and sugar cane. Grandfather himself learned how to refine sugar at Mori no Ie."

He thought they had lost their wealth but didn't know why their fortunes took a downturn. "That's just the way it is in this transient, unpredictable world! I'll bet the Asabas started to sell their fields, bit by bit, because if you ask around, many villagers will say, 'This land here used to belong to Mori no Ie.'"

"What about Yamada's childhood?" I asked.

"My father could have talked forever on that subject but he's been in his grave these past twenty years. One thing he told me stuck in my mind, though. He said Yamada Waka only finished the fourth grade. Isn't it amazing how far she got in this world with so little schooling . . . her picture all over the magazines and newspapers? She must have been a terrific person."

He searched his memory awhile and went on. "I remember one episode when she and her husband came to Kumura. It was around 1910. I must have been in the first or second grade. All the boys at school were in a huddle discussing the red eggplant and the woman from America who was visiting Mori no Ie."

He observed my puzzled expression. "The red eggplant? You don't know what that is? Why, it's a tomato," he announced with an air of triumph. "The tomato was introduced here in the early 1900s. The villagers planted it because it fetched such a high price up in Tokyo. But no one around here ate it. The smell was awful. Besides, it was rumored that the red eggplant could affect the mind, cause death even. Naturally, children were too frightened to go near it. But not that woman from America. She was fearless. She picked up that crazy eggplant and devoured it as if it were a delicacy. I was stupefied. I'll never forget that!"

I asked about Waka's clothing and again he came through.

"Western dress? No, no, she wore a kimono. I expected her to have on a wide hat and something fancy but she wore just a plain kimono. Almost like my mother's," he added. "My friends and I watched her from a distance. We didn't dare get close because we thought she would speak to us in English. In fact, as soon as she started to head towards us we took off through the fields. But that was how country boys behaved."

He said his father once mentioned that Yamada Waka did not have an easy life in America but that he never had understood the implications behind the remark. Someone else had told him that Waka had lived in a place like Yoshiwara. Again there were no details.

Unable to recollect anything more, the old man changed the subject. "Really, like I said, nearly everyone's gone. I'm sure you won't learn anything more than what I've already told you. Go home before it gets dark. On second thought, you don't need an old man's advice. I forget that the trains for Tokyo leave every twenty or thirty minutes. In my day the way people came to Kurihama from Tokyo was by a small steamer that put in at the Kurihama wharf."

With the old man's expressions of esteem for Yamada firmly impressed on my mind, I once more plunged into her works. Knowing a little about her birthplace, some passages in her short stories now took on a new meaning. I began to perceive that Waka had indeed described both her family situation and her own feelings.

I took the interviews, the information I had copied from the family register, my notes on her works and gradually reconstructed Waka's childhood, although in trying to explain why she had gone to America I still felt as if I were trying to scratch the bottom of my foot without taking off my shoe.

Asaba Waka was born on December 1, 1879, at 699 Kumura, Miura County, Kanagawa Prefecture. Her father Kunihisa had been a farmer, traditional, conservative and rather narrow in his views, unable to extend his vision beyond his own village. But he must have been warm and loving since Waka named her grandson after him.

In tracing the Asaba genealogy I discovered that Waka's father had been an adopted son-in-law. Going back a couple of generations, we find a well-to-do farmer, Asaba Risaburō, whose son Chōji inherited the family name and fortune but produced no male heir. In order to continue the Asaba lineage, Chōji went to a nearby village and chose a groom for his daughter Mie. The groom was none other than Kunihisa and Waka was one of the offspring of this union, begun in 1862 at the age of twenty-six when he married his nineteen-year old bride. They had seven children between 1868 and 1886. There were three boys and four girls and Waka was the fifth child, second daughter. Among so many children Waka may have been somewhat neglected, for among other things, it is safe to assume that the Asabas favored their sons. Even though the concept of equality permeated the air, males were given more love and attention than females. The Asaba household would not have been an exception to the norm.

Several passages confirm that Waka, physically well developed and healthy, enjoyed rather atypical forms of recreation for a young girl. For instance, she used to play in the nude in the pond in front of her house or amid the rice paddies. She loved to catch tadpoles, dive after beetles or chase frogs, no matter where they jumped to. The frogs, she skinned, wrapped in leaves, cooked over the hearth, and ate.

For companionship she preferred her kind and generous older sister Yae and her brother Tsunekichi, with whom she had a competitive relationship. Waka missed them both after they started school. There is a short story about a little girl who screamed and kicked and followed her brother and sister because she too wanted to go to school. Annoyed, the older children led her in a strange direction and then ran away. The lost child began to cry in front of a house with a black wooden fence. It was summer and as usual she had no clothes on. She rubbed her hands against the fence and wiped away her tears. Her face and body were smeared in black, as if she had been dumped in a coal bin. Finally a woman passing by suspected from her nudity that she was the child from Mori no Ie and took her home safely.

The incident prompted Kunihisa to seek permission from the principal for his daughter to play in the school yard. Not content with that Waka often slipped into the classroom and sat down quietly next to Yae. Her presence was easily accepted because many children came to school with a younger brother or sister strapped on their back.

In 1886 Waka became old enough for the Kurihama Elementary School. She was overjoyed, usually rose at dawn and urged Tsunekichi to take her to school even though it was still too early. With her natural intelligence she stood at the top of her class from grades one to four. Had she been able to continue she might have led a normal, happy life, albeit an ordinary one.

At that time parents were compelled to give their children four years of schooling. After that they had an option. Many of Waka's friends did have the opportunity to go on but her parents denied her further schooling, since her father believed that "a farmer's daughter only had to learn to write her name and that no good could come out of more education." Waka begged but to no avail. "I can skip one meal a day," she pleaded. But he was adamant and said she was just a child who would soon forget. Her mother tried to console her by offering to teach her how to sew.

Her hopes for an education dashed forever, Waka babysat for her older brother and worked in the fields, planting and weeding alongside her parents, sisters and brothers. In the winter she learned to sew. Of all the many activities, she fondly described making sugar.

In the early autumn after the ripe cane was harvested and stacked under the eaves of the house, a grinding machine with a long bar across the top was brought into the backyard. Waka drove the ox that pulled the contraption until all the

juice was squeezed out of the cane. The grassy-smelling con-
coction was then boiled in a kettle. No one minded when
Waka licked the spoon from time to time.

Once in a while she carried her niece and nephew to the
school yard and listened wistfully to the voices of the children
inside. However, she harbored no grudge against her parents.
On the contrary she remained a devoted and unselfish
creature, as the following story illustrates.

One day a shriveled dirty beggar moved in under the porch
of the Hachiman Shrine. Waka fed her, but the starved
woman asked for more food. The girl brought her leftovers
until her parents found out and gave her a sound scolding.
The story spread and soon the village children were chant-
ing, "Waka of Mori no Ie is really the beggar's daughter."

Certainly she was generous! Generously proportioned, too,
it seems. By the time she was fourteen she was taken for an
adult. Young men were attracted to her. In several stories
Waka refers to a certain Tora-san, a manly looking youth
with bushy eyebrows who is never given a full name. He came
from a poor family, possibly of tenant farmers, and sold fresh
vegetables in Kurihama and neighboring ports or worked at
various menial jobs. A long pole slung over his shoulders,
the lad sometimes waited for Waka until she emerged from
her sewing lesson. But Waka was too shy to respond to his
overtures.

Nevertheless, she cherished the memory of the young man
who was perhaps the first to love her. During those dark years
in America, Tora-san often appeared in her dreams. She
wrote that "He comforted her . . . like a faithful servant he
got down on his knees . . ." and he "was a rare treasure which

she kept in her bosom." Apparently, no one knew about him.

Tora-san's family was no match for the Asabas. Had it been otherwise the young man might have gathered his courage and proposed marriage through some member of his family. How different Waka's life might have been! Or Waka and Tora-san might have defied tradition and formed a romantic liaison. But this was not to be either. The proud, well-entrenched Asabas had other plans for their daughter.

Fate soon intervened and made Waka the wife of another. It was recorded that Waka "married Araki Hichijirō of Yokosuka on August 20, 1896, at the age of sixteen." He was ten years her senior. Very little was ever written about the marriage which suggests that it remained a painful phase in Waka's life.

Hichijirō, as his name implies, was the seventh son. The Arakis' business was not recorded. In any case, since Hichijirō was not the heir, he had to find an independent course, which he did, as one of the many brokers or middlemen employed around Yokosuka's busy naval yard.

His character is revealed in Waka's short story, "A Sullied Flower," published in *Seitō* in 1915. Despite fictitious names there are similarities to Waka's husband. The story centers around a sixteen-year-old country girl who becomes the "victim of her family's sudden decline and of meddlesome relatives."

According to the story, "Before long, the gently inexperienced hand was firmly in the grip of this huge, vulgar man. At the age of ten he lost his father and peddled odds and ends. By fourteen he was able to support his mother. But he was so stingy that within a few years he accumulated a small fortune and was regarded as the richest man in the village. Night and day, he preoccupied himself with making money."

This miser was so distrustful of his own household help that he made separate sleeping arrangements with his new wife. To guard his property, he lived on the second floor of the storehouse while she remained in the shop section of their house.

When the heroine's family was forced to sell their last parcel of land, the husband menaced his wife, warning that he would divorce her if she requested aid for her family. Perhaps like the villain of the story, Hichijirō really was a Scrooge. Waka was probably forced to marry him at sixteen as a result of "the family's sudden decline and of meddlesome relatives." The decline of the Asabas is documented in two of Waka's essays, "A Glimpse at My Youth" and "To Girls Deprived of High School."

No doubt the Asabas loved Waka. Yet, they expected her to marry a rich man who would be of financial assistance to them. But like the husband in "A Sullied Flower," Hichijirō turned out to be a miser. Each time the Asabas asked for money, he must have refused. If he had been the generous type Waka would surely have remained with him and asked nothing more from marriage. By helping her family Hichijirō would have proved that he loved her. But after his rejection of them Waka concluded that he had no affection for her either. Gradually, she drifted away from her husband and gave her heart to her family, particularly to her eldest brother who was struggling to save the family property. In one passage Waka wrote, "I felt compassion and sorrow for my eldest brother who looked haggard because of his overwhelming responsibilities. In order to save a bit of land he had to raise a portion of the large mortgage, but even that was beyond his ability. No wonder my proud brother has lost his vitality."

The passage continues, "I decided that I had to share some of the burden, and once I had made that decision I felt a wonderful sense of self-fulfillment." But behind that resolve was the fierce hatred for a husband who had turned a deaf ear to all of his wife's pleas.

It is conjecture, but I think we can put together a scenario of how Waka might have planned to get money for her family. First, she went to Yokohama to find a job. What happened afterwards is contained in an essay, "To an American Woman," in *Love in Our Society*.

Waka described how in Yokohama she met the wife of a "successful" Japanese businessman. She was eighteen when she encountered this person and was advised to go to America "where men are digging gold from the mines and getting rich, where women earn several times more than a seamstress or housemaid in Japan." The impressionable Waka was easily convinced, perhaps because the woman displayed jewelry and other signs of wealth. Anyway, the woman told her, "If you go to America you'll be rich in just a year or two and you'll surely be able to fulfill your filial duties."

Waka was given a sealed letter which the woman told her to present to her husband as soon as she arrived in America. She left Japan shortly after 1895, when the Sino-Japanese War had ended. On the ship crossing the Pacific the young woman bade her husband a final farewell.

In one of her short stories we find this: "My miserly husband who valued money more than his wife, good-bye. You did not help my brother. But I will rescue him by working hard. I will send him money to rebuild the family. In Japan I was despised for being a woman. But I'll be cared for and well treated in America. And I'll become richer than you are now and return to Kurihama."

The moment Waka set foot ashore she was seized by pimps and sold to a brothel. The wife of the rich, successful Japanese businessman in America had been no more than a procuress out to deceive as many young girls as she could. Waka had fallen into a trap.

I recalled the Karayuki-san of *Sandakan* who were tricked by procurers and their female counterparts into believing that "they could make great salaries as maids." I suspected that Waka left Yokohama for San Francisco under a similar misconception.

The next step was to investigate the kind of men she had encountered and, in general, the sort of life she led. Most important was discovering how she escaped. But that phase of her life was known to two very old people in San Francisco, Kitano Motoji and Izumi Ie. My family agreed that I had to visit the United States. As soon as my mind was made up to go, the burning sunset ceased to haunt my dreams.

Midnight Phone Calls

$\mathcal{I}$ arrived in San Francisco the afternoon of December 3, 1975. Mr. Shimizu had arranged for a guide to help me get around the Bay Area, so I was greeted at the airport by a personable man in his mid fifties who gave his name as Kawase Taiichi. As we headed toward the city I marvelled at the green hedges, lush foliage and spacious boulevards of suburbia and intermittently exchanged small talk with Kawase about Japanese fashions, American life and other general topics. After early winter in Tokyo and a tiring plane trip the warm California sun bolstered my spirits.

"What a shame you've lost such a valuable contact," said Kawase in a calm, matter-of-fact tone.

"What, has something happened?" I asked, not expecting Kawase to bring the conversation around to the purpose of my visit so soon.

"Mr. Kitano died," he replied mechanically, his eyes fixed on the road.

Thoroughly shaken, I froze in my seat, as if ice water had been thrown in my face. "You mean the old man who owned the hotel in Chinatown, Kitano Motoji?"

My voice rose to such a shrill pitch that Kawase was compelled to look my way. "Yes," he said more sympathetically. "And only a few days ago I asked him to help you. Now he's gone. This very morning. Quite suddenly."

I forgot the bright sunshine. I had counted on this interview for so many weeks that it was hard not to feel disappointed. Nervously, I asked whether Izumi Ie was in good health and Kawase nodded affirmatively.

I checked into a nice comfortable room at the Miyako Hotel but spent a restless night, troubled by a strange oppressive uneasiness. Eventually I saw the dawn. Kawase came early to pick me up and I left the hotel without having breakfast. Although I was expected at both the Japanese Consulate General and Shimizu's office, I asked Kawase to drive directly to the Kitano house in Oakland, eighteen miles across the bay from San Francisco.

A short woman, probably in her eighties, her silvery hair tied back in a bun, answered the doorbell. Mrs. Kitano seemed bewildered at first by the appearance of strangers but welcomed us after Kawase explained the reason for my visit. We were shown into the living room where I placed some flowers on a small altar bearing Kitano Motoji's picture. I offered his widow a few words of condolence and was prepared to leave when she ushered us into another room.

"I'll tell you whatever I can just as my husband would have. Although he is dead he would have gone out of his way to help you who have come from so far away to see him." Noticing my reticence, she became more insistent. "I appreciate your sensitivity to my feelings, but please go ahead and ask questions."

I learned that the Kitano Hotel, located near the Chinese-owned shops and brothels in the heart of Chinatown, had been a four-story stucco structure containing numerous small rooms rented on a weekly or monthly basis to a largely Oriental clientele; sometimes blacks checked in. The establishment thrived in the late 1890s.

Among their numerous guests Mrs. Kitano particularly recalled a Japanese sailor from Kyushu who used to stay at their hotel whenever he came to town. He frequented the brothels in the next block and used to enjoy chatting with the Kitanos about his experiences with the Japanese and Chinese girls, a few of whom had come from his hometown, or so he said.

Mrs. Kitano then spoke of an incident involving her daughter Misao. While the child was outside one day playing ball with a friend whose parents managed one of the whorehouses, the ball accidentally rolled into the house. Misao chased it down the hall, catching glimpses as she ran of the tiny rooms furnished with only a bed. The naive girl asked her friend about them, but her questions were ignored. Mrs. Kitano made sure to point out that she herself had never set foot in any of those dens of iniquity, as she referred to them.

She also talked about Cameron House, a haven and rehabilitation center for women who managed to escape the profession. It was run by missionaries and located diagonally across from the Kitano Hotel. There was no contact between the two, but a woman once phoned from Cameron House to complain that a resident of the Kitano Hotel was standing nude in front of his window. "It may be hot out-side," the caller admonished, "but tell your guest to draw the curtains." I had no idea at the time that this Cameron House would become a key to understanding the life of Yamada Waka.

The widow had really nothing unusual to say about the brothels. I suspected that as a women her knowledge of the subject was limited and that her husband might have been able to tell me much more. Anyway, no matter how much I prodded, Mrs. Kitano could not be induced to pronounce the name of Yamada Waka.

By noon my escort and I were back in San Francisco and ready for lunch at the Otafuku Tei. I felt right at home in Japan Center. Except for its cobblestone streets, the entire area replicated things familiar: signs in Japanese, shops sit-ting under black tiled roofs, posts of natural wood and *shōji* screens. At the restaurant I introduced myself to the current owner who was Izumi Ie's adopted daughter. After lunch the daughter phoned her mother and arranged an interview.

It was a ten-minute walk to Izumi's house, an attractive, weather-beaten frame dwelling whose shingles reminded me of layers of bird feathers. Izumi's young niece answered the door and led me upstairs to a sunlit room. The ninety-four-year old woman was leisurely reclining in a chair, clad in a pinkish rose-petalled gown with a long red robe and match-ing slippers. Such an outlandish outfit would have been unthinkable in Japan, even though some older women there had begun to venture into brighter fashions. "But this is

America," I said to myself, "and this is what can happen to first generation immigrants."

The polite thing to do and the best way to begin, I decided, was to direct the conversation to Izumi's early years as a newcomer to America and then talk about the Otafuku Tei. Izumi was soon bubbling over with descriptions of how her small luncheonette, which had once specialized in noodle dishes, prospered and then expanded until there were ten employees. But whenever I asked about the brothels or Yamada, she either changed the subject or stopped talking altogether. I realized that, Americanized as she was, a woman of her generation simply would not discuss certain topics with strangers. For two hours I did my best to elicit information from her. Eventually, I gave up and decided that she really knew nothing about Yamada or any other Ameyuki-san.

I was puzzled. Izumi and Yamada had been practically contemporaries, both immigrants from Japan and both living in San Francisco. It did not make sense unless Izumi's center of activity had been some distance away from Chinatown. I was not satisfied with this conclusion.

It was late afternoon and I had to leave. From the way Izumi repeatedly urged me to stay, I surmised that I had been one of her rare visitors. As I headed towards the door this rather stout old woman rose from her chair and shuffled towards the door to see me off.

Frustration! Another dead end. All the way across the ocean for nothing! Two vital links to Waka's past—so I had assumed—led nowhere. I certainly felt as if the Fates were conspiring against me. The inner voice that had driven me to delve into Yamada Waka's life in the first place seemed to have abandoned me at a very crucial moment. Unsure of my next move, sapped of strength, I lay down to rest and fell asleep from sheer exhaustion, but I awoke after a short nap to see the lights twinkling in the early darkness. I remembered to dial the *Hokubei Mainichi Shimbun*. Luckily, Mr. Shimizu was still there and I hastily left to see him.

We started off by apologizing to each other, I for not coming sooner, he, for the failure of his suggestions. "I shouldn't have advised you to take on this project," he said, and then added, as he scrutinized my crestfallen face, "But don't be dejected. There may be a way out."

He offered to write about me and my work in the newspaper. "I'm sure that some of our readers will contact you," he insisted. He also called the *Nichibei Jiji Shimbun*, a competitor, and convinced the editor to carry the same article.

Two days later, I cautiously allowed myself to hope again as I read, "Yamazaki, a specialist in women's history, is writing the biography of Yamada Waka. But she is in a quandary since an important contact who might have known Yamada when she was a prostitute in San Francisco has recently passed away. Anyone with knowledge of Yamada's past is requested to call Yamazaki at the Miyako Hotel."

All day I waited and waited, refusing to budge from the hotel. But the occasional call I received had nothing to do with Waka. By evening I was tired and nervous. After dinner and a shower I tumbled into bed, tossing and turning, but I fell asleep anyway and the next thing I remembered was the insistent ringing of the phone. "Am I dreaming?" I wondered, dashing to the lamp and the receiver.

"Hello, hello. . ."

"Are you Mrs. Yamazaki . . . Yamazaki Tomoko?" inquired the low, subdued voice of an elderly woman.

"Yes. . ."

"I have to tell you how deeply moved I was during the lecture you gave here on your last visit. And after seeing today's newspaper article, I was very anxious to speak to you."

Expecting her to have information about Waka, I suggested a meeting, but she refused.

"I'm sorry Mrs. Yamazaki. I did not know Yamada Waka personally. My deceased husband once told me that a certain woman from a house of ill repute became famous after she went back to Japan. But surely that's not news to you."

While I was still thinking of an appropriate response, the anonymous voice continued, "Are you listening, Mrs. Yamazaki, because I want to reveal something that no one is ever to know. That's why I won't give you my name and address. You see, I was in Yamada's position a long time ago."

The implication was clear and I urged her to go on.

"I was one of those young girls who were tricked into coming to this country." Her voice faded to a whisper. "I'll explain quickly how it happened. To begin with I was born in the remote mountains of Mie Prefecture. I found work at fifteen as a live-in maid in Nagoya, and one day, while out on an errand, accidentally lost about one yen. I wandered all over the city, frightened by what my master would say. I knew he'd be very angry. By evening I still couldn't choose between returning to my native village or committing suicide. Then a smartly dressed man came along and convinced me to go to America. He didn't have to try very hard. I delivered myself into his hands and he paid for my trip across the ocean. As soon as I got off the boat I was sold to a brothel in Chinatown.

"I had no intention of losing my virginity to a stranger. I struggled until they nearly tortured me to death. In the end I lost and agreed to give myself to Japanese men. Later, I took on Chinese as well. Years passed. Then a Japanese laborer paid off my debts and I was set free. He was ten years older than I. We got married and I've had a normal life ever since. We adopted a child because I couldn't conceive. My husband lived long enough to witness our son's wedding. I'm seventy-seven now and spend my days peacefully with my son and his family." There was a pause and then she said, "I hope the silly chattering of an old woman will be of some use to you. Good night, Mrs. Yamazaki." She ended in a barely audible voice that symbolized the permanent stigma she carried in her heart.

I heard the phone click. In spite of the fact that no one could have heard her, she had been afraid to take a chance before midnight, before making absolutely certain that everyone had gone to bed. Afterwards, I received two more calls, the first from a strange man who said he was in Chinatown working at his job.

"If you want to learn about someone in 'Cisco," he said, "just call on Old Red. People call him 'Red' because he wears red shirts even though he's ninety. He used to gamble, drink and chase after women but he's getting on. Doesn't hear too well anymore. Hmm, come to think of it, maybe you shouldn't depend on his memory either." With that he hung up.

The second caller was a woman who identified herself as Ota Aki, the mother of two sons—a doctor and a lawyer—and an avid reader of the well-known Japanese magazine, *Bungei Shunjū*. I gathered that she was fairly cultured, intelligent and probably elderly.

"I read about Yamada Waka a long time ago," she said. "I advise you to look into the back issues, those of the thirties, of *The American Journal*. Really, you ought to investigate this immediately."

I did, the very next morning. Shimizu knew a great deal about *The American Journal*. It had been the leading Japanese weekly of the decade. Its publisher, Oka Shigeki, not only wrote the articles, but together with his wife, oversaw the distribution.

I was surprised to hear Oka's name mentioned in such circumstances. A socialist opposed to the absolutist trend of the Meiji government, Oka left Japan for the U.S. at the beginning of this century. He was a well-known figure and helped the famous socialist Kōtoku Shūsui to get from Japan to the States. Kōtoku became a hard-core anarchist in America and on his return to Japan was caught by the police and executed in 1911 for lese majesty.

During World War II, Oka, as a staunch believer in democracy, lent a hand to the Allies' propaganda efforts against the Japanese forces in Burma; in fact, the subtitle of his book *Against My Own Motherland* reads, *Pacifist Activities of a Japanese-American*.

I thought of the Oka-Kōtoku friendship that afternoon on my way to the house of Mrs. Oka and her daughter.

The aging woman looked rather well. She could still sew

and was proud of it. Our conversation focused quickly on such socialists as Kōtoku and Sasaki, and then I was shown a photo of a woman whom she said was a daughter of Katayama Sen. Katayama, a graduate of Yale, was associated with the American Communist Party and later played an important role in the Komintern and died in Moscow in 1933.

Mrs. Oka recalled the articles on Yamada Waka her husband had written and published in *The American Journal*, no copies of which were to be found in libraries or universities in the Bay area. It turned out that the only set in existence had been donated to a university, which one, Mrs. Oka could not recall. She was sure that her nephew, who was in Japan on a short business trip, could provide the information. Two days later I met her nephew at his office at the Bank of Tokyo and learned that a complete set of *The American Journal* had been given to the University of California, Los Angeles, library because "Uncle said it would best be preserved in the archives." He phoned UCLA to confirm the presence of the *Journal* and then arranged for a Prof. Lin to meet me at noon the next day at the Los Angeles airport.

It was about an hour's drive to the library. I had no trouble conversing with Prof. Lin. He spoke fluent Japanese. When I arrived, I plunged into the stack of *American Journals* waiting for me on a long table. Finally, "The Story of the Arabian Oyae" unfolded before me. Beginning with the issue dated February 12, 1938, Oka had written five articles on Yamada Waka. These he published in conjunction with her lecture tour of the United States, which had begun in the autumn of 1937 under the sponsorship of a Japanese woman's magazine.

It was all there just as the midnight caller had promised. I received permission to photocopy the articles and returned to San Francisco that night. On the plane I studied Oka Shigeki's incredible account of Waka's past. Of special interest to me was a postscript which he had intended for Waka.

Now that I have finished this series, I must apologize to Yamada Waka, for I am truly sorry to have made the past public, it being in such sharp contrast to her present greatness. However, I wanted only to tell the truth, to prevent the circulation of lies and false rumors after her death. Please believe me, Mrs. Yamada, I did not intend to hurt you. One of my objectives was to show our readers that a person can overcome a wrong turn and achieve greatness, but it takes your kind of courage and determination.

I also hoped to reach out to those women who are still trapped in the situation you once were in. If you find any mistakes in the story, Mrs. Yamada, I would appreciate hearing from you despite the pain it might cause you to recollect the past. I know that your generous and understanding nature will help you realize that I was not motivated by any malice whatsoever.

As I pondered the postscript it occurred to me that Oka had been motivated to write Waka's story by something deep and personal, something well beyond a concern for accurate reporting. I recalled a certain essay written by Oka's brother which had been included in the volume *Against My Own Motherland*. "Memoirs of my Brother," as the essay was called, recounts in detail Shigeki's adventures as a young journalist

for a Tokyo newspaper. One of his favorite activities had been
to help prostitutes escape from brothels. His involvement in
this idealistic cause may have been encouraged by a Japanese
judicial decision at that time which declared debts owed by
prostitutes to their pimps to be null and void, a decision which
led many geisha and whores to try to get away. Shigeki once
rushed over to his cousin's house to borrow a kimono so that
a prostitute could disguise herself. The successful getaway of
the Arabian Oyae no doubt awakened in Oka Shigeki his
own youthful past.

Thanks to his articles I began to grasp the intricacies of
Waka's life. Two surprising facts emerged that caused me to
reevaluate the situation: Waka had landed in Seattle, not
in San Francisco, and Yamada Kakichi had not been her
savior. Oka said it had been a journalist by the name of Tachii
Nobusaburō. At first I questioned his facts. People in Japan
and elsewhere believed that Waka had been rescued by
Kakichi in San Francisco. But I could not dismiss Oka's account. His version was written while Waka was visiting the
United States and he specifically asked her to advise him if
there were mistakes to be corrected in the story. Also, Oka's
version explained why I could not find anyone in San Francisco who had known Waka. Given all the variations and
possibilities, it now seemed likely that someone other than
Kakichi had helped Waka escape.

Snowy Seattle

A freezing town in the far north. Except for the cleared runways, all around lay a thick white blanket of snow. More flakes danced in the air, and the stinging cold pricked my skin like sharp needles. I never expected to visit this unfamiliar city, but there I was, shivering in my fur coat and feeling as gloomy as the weather since I knew virtually no one in Seattle. I missed San Francisco where I could find my way around a bit and had Shimizu to rely on. It had been a short flight, only two hours, but very dramatic, the scenery swiftly changing from flat, sunny orange groves to the high peaks of the Cascade Range and then to wintry Seattle.

I checked into the Olympic Hotel in the center of town and made plans to visit the office of the Japan Association the next morning. Luck was with me. President Mihara Genji was in and immediately introduced me to the secretary of the organization. Kageyama Noboru, who had been born and raised in Seattle, had at some point decided to settle in Japan but then, for reasons unknown to me, eventually returned to his birthplace.

Kageyama and I set out to talk with men in their eighties and nineties. None of those we met had known Yamada Waka personally, although all of them had heard of her and some recalled that she had been mixed up in some "shady business." At first I suspected that the men simply did not want to open up in the presence of Kageyama. I would have liked to speak to each one in private, but there was no opportunity and their reticence continued to form a barrier. No man, I thought later, would admit to frequenting brothels. Besides Kageyama, there was another inhibition: children and grandchildren were often listening to our conversation.

Gradually I changed my mind. More than seventy years had passed since Yamada had been in that city. A man of eighty would have been under ten; a ninety-year old would not have been over twenty. In fact, most of the men had not even emigrated to the United States until after the turn of the century.

Moving around the city from one interview to the next, it seemed as if Yamada's past lay buried under mounds of snow and no one could hope to dig it out. But I finally got a break. Kageyama introduced me to a friendly ninety-two year old, the oldest among Seattle's Japanese-Americans. Tamesa Uhachi was not the least bit reluctant to discuss Yamada.

"Welcome to Seattle, Yamazaki-san," he began. "You've come a long way. Cold, eh? I remember I was shocked by the terrible weather when I first got here. But if you stay even a short time you'll discover all the good things about this place. Anyway, time to have something hot to warm you up. You too, Mr. Kageyama. Here's the sugar. Go ahead, help yourselves to some tea.

"So, you'd like to know about Yamada Waka. I would never have dreamed in a million years that someone would come from Japan just to ask about her. I wonder how old she is. Maybe I should find out if she's still alive?"

"Waka is dead," I replied, adding the pertinent details.

"Is that so! Well, no one lives forever. She and I were only a few years apart. She was older though. So she went to heaven at seventy-eight. Not exactly young. But really, have twenty years gone by already since she died? Maybe I've lived too long. A good thing though, huh? Otherwise I wouldn't be around to tell you about her.

"From the start you have to realize that what I know about her is limited. We only exchanged a few words now and then. And not behind a red curtain. It didn't have anything to do with sex. I was around nineteen when I met her, very poor. I couldn't afford to go to the red light district. And if I had had the money I couldn't have gotten to the Arabian Oyae. She was reserved for whites only."

He said that he hadn't known her real name then, only her nickname, the Arabian Oyae. Probably no one knew her real name. Women in that business—men too, for that matter—never revealed their names or told where they were born. A woman from Hiroshima would say she was from Osaka and one from Nagasaki might let on that she was from Kyoto. It was natural for a person in such an occupation to try and hide his or her past. With a name it was easy enough, although dialects might betray a person's origins.

Often there were no records of a person's entry into the country, so nothing could be learned from the consulate or immigration office. In the early 1900s Seattle and Vancouver were the frontiers of America and Canada. Rarely did a customs inspector or immigration officer appear on the docks. Sometimes, a person without a passport tied his personal belongings on top of his head, then jumped overboard and swam ashore to safety.

"But getting back to Yamada. I didn't know her name then, and it was another twenty years before I heard rumors about a famous Japanese social critic who once lived in Seattle. It happened one day while I was looking through a Japanese woman's magazine my wife borrowed. I saw a photo that certainly resembled the Arabian Oyae, although the woman in the magazine wore a conservative kimono and looked older than the Arabian Oyae. But I had no doubts it was her. What a surprise! I couldn't believe that a shameless woman had become so famous."

Tamesa had met Yamada while he was working as a delivery boy. That was around 1903 when he was nineteen or twenty. He told us those were tough times, for he was the eighth and last child of a poor farmer who lived on the island of Oshima in the Inland Sea. Life there was tranquil, but no paradise. They had sweet potatoes which they grew themselves but not much of anything else. Sooner or later Tamesa knew he would have to leave home. Then his father fell seriously ill, and no doctor would come to treat him since they were so poor. He was eighteen and knew he had to help out in some way.

He heard that the former principal of his elementary school

had moved to Seattle, opened a variety store, and was looking for a young man from the village to help him. Tamesa made his way to Seattle. It was mid winter 1899, and he still remembers feeling frozen to the bone. But by the time he arrived the job had been filled.

He continued his recital. "I had my troubles. Couldn't speak English, no skills. Orientals were discriminated against. I did hard labor and slowly learned English. I finally landed a job with the Orient Express. They had customers all over the city and needed a delivery boy. The Sato Grocery was one of their customers. And that's where the story really begins."

Sato's wife, a neat, dainty-looking woman, had once been behind the red curtain on King Street. Her old friends from there used to come to the grocery to shop and gossip. Yamada was among them. Tamesa used to see her occasionally while making a delivery. She was a stout, hefty woman, rather dark. She dressed more conservatively than other women in the profession and never wore make up—at least, not that he'd ever seen. She and Mrs. Sato were very good friends and used to talk to each other familiarly, as if they were sisters. Both of them came from Kanagawa Prefecture. Immigrants from the same place tended to become friends pretty fast in America.

"I used to call her 'Big Sister' because I didn't know how to address a woman like that. Sometimes we spoke about inconsequential things like the weather. Waka was not the talkative type, though. She was different from the others, maybe because she was polite and not pretentious. If I can trust my memory I believe she belonged to the Eastern Hotel."

The Eastern was for Caucasians. On King Street, it was, which was the combat zone in those days. There were dance halls, shooting galleries, gambling and billiard halls, and at one end of the street, the brothels: Aloha House, Tokyo House, Diamond House, Yokohama House, Eastern Hotel and so on. Each whorehouse catered to certain types. The women lived elsewhere and commuted, coming to work around four or five in the afternoon. An ugly or unpopular woman had to arrive earlier, say by 11 in the morning. Work was usually over by midnight, except when the woman had an overnight client. Tamesa used to help the women move their stuff from one place to another. There was never anything big, just a valise, a wicker basket, a few packages. They didn't own much. The pimp would bargain for the moving fee and then oversee the proceedings.

"I don't suppose you know much about a pimp," Tamesa offered. "He lives off a woman and he's hard to get rid of. But he's a necessary institution. There are times when he's the woman's only protection. He usually gambles and is damn stingy, tries to squeeze all the money he can out of a woman. I knew of women who tried to escape. When they got caught, the pimp would hit, kick or even torture them."

Later on there were sanctuaries for women to run to, and the lucky woman who managed to get to one was freed from misery, at least in some cases. Some pimps hired professional killers to go after the woman. Tamesa said he knew of women who had been murdered—just disappeared and were never heard from again. Many a woman was kidnapped and brought into the country to serve as a prostitute. If she disobeyed the pimp, she could wind up dead. And her murder was usually committed in a brutal way, perhaps as a warning to others. To conceal the evidence, the body might be cut into small pieces. A machine ground up the flesh and internal organs while the bones were dissolved with a chemical solution and flushed into the sewers.

"Waka must have had some pimp around her. But I have no idea who he was or what he was like," he continued. "I vaguely remember her saying that she had once been in Alaska—no, no, I heard that from someone else. A certain Kosaku Sakamaki, one of the bosses in a salmon fishery, said Waka had probably been shipped from Seattle to the Klondike. You know when gold mining began everyone rushed to get rich. White and yellow, they ran straight up there. And they needed plenty of women, too. I don't remember just when I stopped seeing Waka at Sato's. I once heard that the Arabian Oyae had escaped and that the pimp was chasing her. But maybe that was some other woman."

I interrupted to ask if he had ever heard of Tachii Nobusaburō, the man who was supposed to have helped Waka get away; but he could not recall the name. He offered to show me where the women used to live.

"King Street has changed over the years but I'll take you there anyway. Kageyama might also be interested. But let's have some more tea and get real warm before we go out."

While we drank our tea Tamesa told us that King Street ran right through Chinatown. The red light district in San Francisco had also been in Chinatown.

It had stopped snowing by the time we set out. As Kageyama drove us through the snowy streets, the city seemed much cheerier now that the sun was shining again.

King Street in Seattle. The Eastern Hotel stood on the site
of the building in the left foreground.

Seattle's Chinatown stretched around the harbor and included Main, Jackson and Weaver streets. The buildings were
mostly three to five stories high with businesses—many are
restaurants—like the Tai Tung, Wan Young, Sun Ya and so
on on the ground floor. Most were Chinese. After an hour's
leisurely stroll we reached the intersection of King Street and
Fifth Avenue.

"Look over there," exclaimed Tamesa, pointing to a red
brick building housing a Chinese restaurant and bar. "That's
where Waka used to be." He smiled boyishly.

It hit me like a thunderbolt! The former site of the Eastern
Hotel. I stood there for several minutes, rooted to the spot,
unable to move, although I sensed people were looking at
me strangely. What a fantastic transformation had taken
place! There had been no white settlement of Seattle prior

to the middle of the 19th century. Then, for several decades a small population prospered on the lumbering industry. In the 1890s, as ocean port and rail center, it burgeoned into one of the most important cities on the West Coast. Still, like many a frontier city, Seattle remained a hunting ground for adventurers, men who searched for instant success and needed liquor and women. Naturally, bars and brothels flourished. But the prostitutes were generally Oriental.

I had read Takeuchi Kojirō's *History of Japanese Immigration to the Northwest Coast of the U.S.*, published in 1929. According to the author, the first immigration of Japanese prostitutes took place in 1887 with the inauguration of the Yokohama-Vancouver voyage. In the beginning only a handful of unfortunate Japanese women crossed the Pacific. Eight years later, the number had risen to six thousand a year. Brothels were shabby wooden structures resembling the flimsy sets built for Western movies, and they actually did have red curtains, as Tamesa mentioned. All the windows must have been covered with those red curtains.

Back in my room at the Olympic Hotel that evening, I watched a flood of neon lights glittering across the snow and then began to reread some of Yamada's works. I studied each and every word and still found no reference to her life in Seattle, not even a disguised allusion to the Eastern Hotel. In one vague passage in the essay, "To an American Woman," there was mention of Victoria. "Going through the whirlpool of life, like autumn leaves blown about by the wind, I was carried on a boat to a harbor on the West Coast. I knew nothing of your country, its places, its customs. I landed in Victoria."

Victoria, British Columbia, at the southern end of Vancouver Island, is sixty miles north of Seattle. No doubt Waka was set ashore in Victoria and then sold to a pimp in Seattle rather than to one hundreds of miles farther south in San Francisco. It made sense. Historians have noted that Canada was more liberal than the U.S. in its immigration policies. Not only that, immigration officers were known to sometimes look the other way and let white slavers bring their women to America through Vancouver and Victoria. I decided it was reasonable to assume that Yamada left Yokohama and landed in Victoria before going to Seattle. Yet, she probably thought it unwise to mention Seattle directly and allude to the years she spent there.

In another essay dated January, 1914, "Myself and My Surroundings," Waka wrote as follows.

> When I emerged from the underground, I was burning with hatred for people, especially for men. I kept wondering what I could do to get revenge on those devils who'd taken advantage of a poor woman and had sucked her blood. I thought of pouring gasoline on their heads and setting them afire. Fighting those men to avenge the poor suffering women—it was a fantasy that filled me with courage. Later, whenever I met a woman who cried because she was being abused by a man, I felt like fighting for her.

The reader unfamiliar with Waka's early life would find such a passage melodramatic and would fail to grasp the implications. But now I understood what Waka meant by men being devils who sucked women's blood and I felt compassion for the woman who wanted to pour gasoline on their heads and set them afire. Waka must have spent many a day behind the red curtain suffering from abuse and fantasizing her revenge. The deeper the pain, the more her reluctance to put in writing the precise name and place of misery. Her fantasy helped divert her hatred and kept her from exploding.

Tachii Nobusaburō

$\mathcal{B}$y the early 1900s Japanese newspapers had proliferated in Seattle. Among them were the *Seattle Shūhō*, *Seikoku Shimpō* and *Hokubei Jiji*. As described by Oka, the editor and manager of the Seattle office of another of these, the *Sekai Shimbun*, was a tall, handsome, outgoing man who sported a mustache. Tachii Nobusaburō was thirty-one years old, some five or six years Yamada's senior, and educated. He especially admired Chinese classics and composed poems and essays in the Chinese style under the pen name Kenshōkaku.

Rumor had it that he was the third son of an old well-established family which had once administered a feudal estate near Nagoya. Tachii himself never spoke about his past in Japan, nor did Oka give any hint as to why this well-bred man had to take a job as a journalist in a remote region of a foreign country. But there he was in Seattle in 1900.

The circumstances under which he came to know the Arabian Oyae remain obscure. Assuming she catered to whites exclusively, it is unlikely that Tachii was one of her clients. On the other hand, he may have met her in the red light district while covering a story. Whatever the case, he fell madly in love with her and plotted her escape from the Eastern Hotel when he could no longer bear to have her sleep with other men. The pimps would not have willingly freed Yamada unless her debt to them had been paid in full. Tachii probably did not have that kind of money, but he figured he could eventually find work in San Francisco, where the *Sekai Shimbun* had its home office. First Yamada's escape had to be carefully planned down to the last detail. A prostitute in those frontier days, as Tamesa pointed out, was valued no more than any other commodity, perhaps less, so if Yamada were caught trying to run away, chances are she would have been brutally tortured.

Something unforeseen interfered with Tachii's plan. While he was on the phone, his conversation with Yamada was overheard as a result of crossed wires. Furuya Masajirō, owner of a variety goods store with a reputation as both a successful businessman and successful racketeer, listened in and learned that one of the King Street women and her lover were preparing their getaway. The Japanese community in Seattle was small, and Furuya had only to make a guess to know the names of the the people involved.

"Excuse me," broke in Furuya. "The lines got crossed and I couldn't help overhearing. Mr. Tachii, I'd like to talk to you. Come to my office this evening and don't worry about a thing. I'll take care of everything. Just leave it to me."

Tachii recovered from his momentary shock and agreed to see Furuya. Meanwhile, suspicious of the man's intentions, he and Waka got ready to leave Seattle by carriage that same night. Of course, it was Tachii who helped Yamada escape from the Eastern by making the rope out of bedsheets. But apparently no one ever knew of Tachii's existence, since she never spoke of him to anyone.

San Francisco, 860 miles to the south, was their destination. After dark they set out for Portland, about one-fifth of the distance. Money became an immediate problem. Tachii left hurriedly, without adequate funds, but it was risky for him to stop and look for a job in Portland. He decided to take a gamble. He hid Waka in an inn and returned to Seattle alone. But he was immediately seized by the owner of the

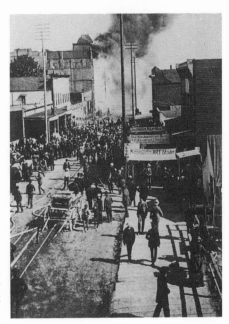

Seattle shortly after the turn of the century. The view here is looking south on Front Street.

Eastern and his cohorts who threatened him at pistol point: either he paid Waka's debts or brought her back. Or else.

Tachii had only his wits to keep him alive. He tried reasoning with the pimps, arguing that nothing could be gained by killing him. He convinced them that he had a scheme to get hold of some money.

Competition was keen among the Japanese newspapers and at times the rivalry became quite heated, particularly between the *Seikoku Shimpō* and a newspaper called *Nihonjin*. There was not only bitterness but personal animosity. The *Seikoku Shimpō* criticized its competitor for the quality of its news coverage and attacked the owners of the Toyo Trading Company, who were the publishers of the *Nihonjin*. Toyo sued the *Seikoku* for libel and won damages in court but sought additional revenge by enticing a shady character named Gonta to break into the *Seikoku* plant. Gonta ransacked the plant and damaged the linotype machine, forcing the newspaper to shut down. He and his cronies were caught in the act and sent to jail.

Tachii had written up the incident and he suggested to the pimps that he go to Gonta and offer to negotiate with Toyo on his behalf. The pimps agreed and they themselves set up the Toyo-Tachii rendezvous. Tachii succeeded in squeezing the bail money out of Toyo. But he ran off with it, evading the pimps who now, twice deceived, redoubled their efforts to get back their property.

The reporter used this unexpected windfall for the purchase of two boat tickets from Portland to San Francisco, and before long he and Yamada were at sea. Their boat sailed down the Columbia River and made a short stopover at the deepwater port of Astoria. From there it proceeded directly to San Francisco. The voyage took four days and they arrived safely.

Yamada Waka might then have given up her professional name of Arabian Oyae and lived happily ever after with the newspaperman who had jeopardized his career, but subsequent events took a turn that defies the imagination.

There are two accounts, with minor discrepancies, of what happened after their arrival in San Francisco, one by Oka, and the other in Takeuchi's *History of Japanese Immigration to the Northwest Coast of the United Sates*.

According to Oka, the couple checked into the Ōhisoya Inn on Stockton Street. How much time passed is not known, but soon thereafter, Tachii had a talk with the owner and then tried to persuade Yamada to go back to the profession she had just escaped from. She ended up in a brothel called the Wakamatsuya, located somewhere around Grant Street and California Avenue in the red light district. Tachii took some $150.00 from Waka's earnings.

Takeuchi wrote that the name of the brothel was the Sakuraya and that the amount Tachii took from Yamada was around $300.00. In any event, the important issue was Tachii's character. Did he ever really love Yamada or had he intended all along to take her away from Seattle only to make money on her elsewhere?

It was only a matter of a few days before Yamada disappeared from the brothel without leaving a trace. The owner of the Wakamatsuya thought Tachii had been involved with her disappearance and rushed over to the Ōhisoya Inn. Tachii was there, in his room, but protested that he had no knowledge of her whereabouts. He was not believed and once again the pimps beat him up. In fact, Tachii had told the truth.

No details are available. The couple may have been anxious to settle down to marriage and a normal life after the risks and intrigues of their recent adventure, but funds ran out, quarreling increased, and a gap grew between them as differences in expectations surfaced. Perhaps Tachii had asked Yamada to work awhile at the brothel until he found a steady job to support her properly. She may have agreed while harboring a grudge. In fact, she may have despised Tachii for compelling her to go back to prostitution, and at the same time she may have still loved him and wished to marry him. In any case, she very likely decided to escape without telling him. Disillusionment and humiliation probably convinced her that it was best to go it alone.

This is all conjecture, of course. Other scenarios and motives are possible but later events give credence to the above. What is known is that Yamada made her way to the Presbyterian Mission House, later called Cameron House, located at 920 Sacramento Street.

Cameron House

Cameron House was the bane of the pimps and an oft-dreamed-of haven for young girls gone astray. It was founded in the autumn of 1874, one year after a Presbyterian missionary returned to San Francisco from China and reported to his mission board that thousands of Chinese girls were being secretly shipped to the West Coast and forced into prostitution. He urged his audience to save them. The board soon agreed that teaching Christian ways to those in their midst took priority over sending missionaries abroad. Before long, donations pouring in from all over the country enabled these good samaritans to rent the second floor of an apartment house. The number who sought refuge grew quickly, and the need for larger quarters was met two years later with the purchase of a 25-room house on Sacramento Street. The first director was Miss S. H. Cummings. She was followed by Miss N. Culbertson and Miss Donaldina Cameron. The settlement house deservingly bears the name of the latter.

The activities at Cameron House under the devoted leadership of Donaldina Cameron are detailed in a fascinating book by Lorna Logan. It seems that from the day Cameron started at the age of twenty-five as Culbertson's assistant, she proved to be a woman of courage and daring. Within a few days of her arrival, her mettle was tested when a corner of the settlement house was blasted by dynamite, no doubt by pimps taking revenge for the loss of their women. Cameron, the daughter of Scottish immigrants, was neither frightened nor intimidated, and decided then and there to dedicate herself to the task of rescuing young Oriental women from brothels.

The pimps called her the "White Witch." Escorted by only a policeman—often bought off by the pimps—she used to march fearlessly into the red light district like a swallow swooping through a flock of vultures, enter the brothels, and demand to see the birth certificates and passports of the girls. When necessary she resorted to physical force to make the pimps bring out the girls. Those under twenty-one or without a passport were removed by the police and taken to Cameron House for rehabilitation.

Swift and tenacious, she was no less quickwitted. Receiving a phone call for help from a girl in Sacramento, Cameron drove there, parked her carriage in front of the brothel, leaving one door open, then hurried inside, identified her caller, grabbed the girl's hand and rushed her into the carriage. At a hotel that night a stranger appeared and offered to help them escape by boat. Cameron, suspecting he had been sent by the pursuing pimps, kept her wits about her. She pretended to accept his proposal, thereby distracting him long enough for her and the girl to slip out the back door and get away.

In her twenty long years of service at Cameron House, Donaldina Cameron freed and rehabilitated more than five hundred young women. Even after she resigned as director, she continued to work on their behalf for another twenty-five years. By the time she retired at seventy, the savior of countless otherwise lost souls was adored as "Lao Mo," a Chinese expression meaning "the Great Mother."

How Yamada Waka discovered the existence of the Great Mother and her house is not clear. Perhaps she had heard of Cameron in Seattle, in which case it was pure luck that Tachii chose to go to San Francisco. On the other hand she might have learned about the settlement house from the women at the Wakamatsuya, which brings us back to the subject of Tachii. The pimps eventually believed his story and were satisfied when Tachii handed over every cent he had taken from Yamada. Both he and she were then off the hook as far as the pimps were concerned, but Tachii remained in a terrible state. Bereft of a career, the trust of others and his girlfriend, he grew even more desperate. He heard from the pimps that Yamada had gone to Cameron House and immediately went there himself to try and see her. Day after day he pleaded with Donaldina Cameron to see his fiancee, as he called Waka. But each time he was turned away.

"You sold Waka to the Wakamatsuya. She will never see the likes of you again," Miss Cameron told him. When he persisted, she added, "Of course, we prefer that she have nothing to do with you. But it is really she herself who refuses to see you."

He still hung around, hoping that Yamada would change her mind. It is hard to say how often he begged Cameron

Donaldina Cameron at the age of twenty-five, when she was just at the beginning of her career of rescuing fallen women.

The second Cameron House, originally called the Presbyterian Mission House for Chinese Girls, was destroyed in the 1906 earthquake.

to arrange a meeting. Eventually his tenacity paid off. He found out that Waka and a few Chinese girls visited a house on Sutter Street three times a week. Tachii went there.

Cameron insisted that the girls learn new skills so that they could someday lead independent and useful lives. She herself taught them sewing and cooking. For embroidery, there was a certain Japanese clergyman on Sutter Street. Sakabe Tasaburō not only instructed the women but also sold their products for them. Tachii hoped that Sakabe, as a fellow countryman, would be sympathetic to his plight. But Sakabe knew all about Tachii and turned him down.

Matters came to a head one day when Tachii arrived threatening to kill himself if he were refused again. The anguished and tormented man poured out his feelings of love, but Sakabe refused to take him seriously. Neither did Yamada, who must have overheard the conversation from the next room.

Without warning, Tachii put his hand in his pocket and declared, "This is the last time I'm going to beg you. Will you let me see her?"

"I'm sorry. I cannot," came the reply in a tone that Tachii knew spelled finality.

In an instant he produced a small flask and gulped down its contents. The astonished minister screamed and rushed to grab the object. It was too late. Tachii groaned and collapsed on the floor. Hearing the commotion, the girls burst in. Yamada cried profusely and hovered over her former lover. By the time the doctor arrived, the tragic life of the young journalist had been extinguished.

In his pocket was a will requesting a proper burial; it was

addressed to Washizu Sekima, one of his friends, another journalist who had come to the United States in 1894 and worked
for the *Shin Sekai Shimbun* and *Sōkō Jiji* before starting his
own magazine, *Taiheiyō*. Washizu arranged for a simple
funeral and Tachii was laid to rest.

Why did Yamada react so coldly to the man who had loved
her, had sacrificed his career, indeed, thought so little of life
without her that he ended his own? What went wrong after
Seattle? Seventy years later, it is impossible to reconstruct
the past from the materials now available. In the end the
reader must draw his own conclusions.

In my opinion, Tachii truly loved Yamada and sent her
to the Wakamatsuya as a last resort. He had convinced
himself that he had no other means of getting money. It is
quite possible that Tachii had been threatened by gangsters

The Street of the Gamblers in
San Francisco's Chinatown as
it appeared in the late 19th century.

who had followed him from Seattle, and the only way out was to pay back the money. No doubt he was stunned when he found out that she had run away. But after her repeated refusals to see him, he must have realized that she was lost to him forever. If he had only wanted to attract attention, as some have suggested, he would not have taken the full dose of poison, nor would he have prepared his will. It seems to me that his death was not the final posturing of an exhibitionist, but rather the last act of a desperate and lonely lover.

As for Yamada, despite the lack of tangible evidence, I conclude (based on her writings) that she did not love Tachii, at least not enough to forgive him for sending her to the Wakamatsuya. Waka tended to write about her experiences and relationships with people in a vague fashion with no specific mention of actual places and people; yet, inferences can be made. It is speculation on my part, but it is not hard to imagine that the following episode from the essay, "Mother," really occurred between Tachii and herself after their hasty flight from Seattle.

I was sitting on a small boat in the middle of the lake on a very dark night. The only light came from the shimmering stars. Angered by my stubbornness, my companion suddenly threatened to kill me with his pistol. I knew I was too far away from civilization to cry out for help. Had I capsized the boat I would have drowned because I could not swim. So I sat perfectly still, leaned back against the thwart, clasped my hands, and closed my eyes. I became resigned to whatever fate was in store for me. He placed a handkerchief over my eyes and let me feel the barrel of his pistol. It was at that point that I recalled something my father once told me. 'If you are innocent, the gods will be with you. Whatever happens is the will of the gods,' so I calmly waited for their will to manifest itself, and it did. They let me live.

Somewhere between Seattle and Portland Tachii must have begged Yamada to have intercourse and was refused. Not once but repeatedly. Irritated and furious with her, he may have rented a boat and considered committing double suicide (first killing her, then himself) with the pistol he was carrying in case of difficulties with their pursuers. If she had screamed for help or jumped into the water, Tachii might have fired. Knowing her character, it is more than likely that she remained quiet and meditated. Angrier than ever because Yamada proved to be the stronger, Tachii must have thrown the weapon into the water.

He was handsome, intelligent and possessed a cultivated taste for Chinese poetry. Why indeed did Yamada fail to respond to this fine man's passionate love?

There is the point of view that Yamada spurned Tachii precisely because she loved him. She knew that a gentleman married to a woman who had been in the profession would be ostracized from society. But I do not share this opinion. Once again I base my perspective on Yamada's writings. I refer to passages in "Myself and My Surroundings" to substantiate the view that Yamada nurtured an intense hatred of men, so much so that she wished to pour gasoline on their heads and set them afire. She fantasized that she led a fight against men. She felt that female ghosts, dressed in white funeral shrouds, came out of their graveyard to join the battle on her side. Tachii had promised to help her escape from the hell of the Eastern Hotel. Yamada accepted his aid, believing that he would be gentle and undemanding; she wanted more than anything else to escape from sexual slavery. However, when Tachii turned out to be overbearing and insistent, like other men, she had only one desire—to escape forever from all men. And that is precisely why she fled to Cameron House.

Their relationship was founded to some extent on a misunderstanding. Tachii, the romantic but unstable lover, did not really understand Yamada, who had no choice but to use whatever means available to free herself. After her years in the Eastern Hotel, she could not have behaved in a normal, loving fashion. She simply could not respond immediately to Tachii's overtures, however sincere.

Unfortunately, Tachii did not understand the rejection. For weeks he wavered between hope and despair. He could not commit suicide in Portland, so they arrived safely in San Francisco, but then he grew furious with her when she still remained cold and unloving. It was possibly an act of revenge, of which he himself was unconscious, when he encouraged her to sell herself to the Wakamatsuya. Or he may have known in his heart that he was being hypocritical when he told her he needed time and money to set their lives on a normal track. In any event, despite this shady side of his character, it is difficult not to feel compassion for the young man who loved a fallen woman and threw away his life for her.

Yamada Kakichi

*W*hen I got back to San Francisco a week later the golden oranges had ripened. My first thought was to visit Cameron House. Kawase arranged for this by contacting an elder of the Presbyterian Church, and we went there the next day.

Standing out among the white modern houses on hilly Sacramento Street was the stately brick mansion at number 920. I looked around and considered where I was—right in the middle of Chinatown. In Japan, it is usual to deliberately locate rehabilitation facilities in sparsely populated areas, both to help the women to be free from unnecessary temptations and to shield them from the curious and the prejudiced. But Cameron House was established right there in the red light district, exposed to all sorts of dangers, not the least of which were the pimps who were in striking range to recover their women or to take revenge. Donaldina Cameron was not afraid of them. From Cameron House she could easily send messages of freedom to girls inside the brothels.

Five steps led up to the entrance. A copper plate on the left bore the inscription "Donaldina Cameron House"; above the entrance itself, it said, "Occidental Board Presbyterian Mission House" and there was a welcoming branch of an evergreen tree. Above the small receptionist's window was a sign in Chinese saying "Cameron House, built by the Presbyterian Church." Beyond that was yet another heavy door to be entered.

I pressed the bell. A Chinese-American in his early thirties greeted us. Kamata Iwao, our guide, requested permission to look through the house and to see the Cameron House publications from the early 1900s. The young man said he was not sure what we wanted but let us in.

Downstairs, a few Christmas decorations, a reminder of the approaching holiday season, offset the somber atmosphere of a prayer enclosure with tiny partitions. Upstairs seemed no more cheerful. A number of narrow, dark corridors led to the individual rooms. To my surprise, our guide opened one of the doors to reveal a lovely, bright nine-by-twelve all white room where light streamed in through a bay window.

This was not the original building. In fact, it was the fourth Cameron House, constructed in 1930. The second had been destroyed in the 1906 earthquake.

We found a complete set of carefully preserved original newsletters. These had been written over the years by various staff members and distributed to the benefactors of the mission house as a means of keeping them up to date on the mission's activities. I was presented with copies of the newsletters written between 1900 and 1905.

At the Miyako Hotel that night I sat engrossed while I

searched out the sections of the newsletters that mentioned Asaba Waka's name. Once in a while I noticed Donaldina Cameron's signature on an article. Several hours later I had a clearer picture of past events.

After Tachii's death Yamada obediently submitted to Cameron's tutelage. She received vocational and religious instruction, the latter intended to foster a spirit of self-reliance. In her essay "Love and Marriage," Yamada wrote about herself in this period as follows.

I was not accustomed to reading as a child. In fact, the Bible was the first book I really read. Until then, I lived in chaotic darkness, without direction, moving only where my toes pointed. The more I studied the Bible, the more the thick mist in front of me lifted. Finally, I saw the dawn.

Specifically, it was the concept of equality under God that inspired Waka and gave her a sense of optimism. She herself expressed it in another essay, "Love in Our Society."

I fled into a sort of nunnery to escape the devouring male beasts. There I came in contact with a book I had always believed was reserved for a certain class: the Bible. When I read that there was a God ruling the universe and that under Him every creature was equal, I gazed up at the sky. Joy and yearning filled my heart. I forgot about the earth. The lamb that had been pushed around by cruel beasts suddenly felt protected by Almighty God. My thirst for direction and meaning was quenched. The stronger I grew, the more I drank out of the fountain of God's love. I began to feel an immense warmth towards all of Nature's creatures. I also acquired the courage to fight evil.

Newsletter #31 (1904) stated that several girls were awaiting baptism and confirmation, among them "Asaba Waka, who has been with us for the past eighteen months and has been of invaluable help to us as an interpreter." This referred to the fact that Cameron sometimes snatched Japanese girls right at the harbor and immediately needed a translator. The same newsletter went on to applaud Waka's confidence and zeal. "We had always hoped to produce a girl who could teach the newcomers. Asaba Waka is certainly one of the brightest and the most dependable. Because of her unhappy experiences, she possesses a true sense of compassion for others. Every morning she invites the girls to sit by her side while she reads the Bible. Afterwards, she and the teacher, Miss Garrity, give English lessons." It seems she was baptized by Rev. Sakabe.

December 10, 1905, and another tribute to Yamada. "The reason for our success is largely due to the efforts of some Chinese and Japanese girls, particularly the one who acts as our interpreter."

Yet all was not rosy for her. Since she had not gone beyond the fourth grade, certain Chinese expressions caused her difficulty, and she could not handle theories and abstractions even in her mother tongue. Her English consisted of simple, stock everyday phrases. The Cameron House staff noticed her frustration and decided to enroll her in Yamada's English School on Bush Street. The institution was run by Yamada Kakichi, who was owner, teacher and caretaker.

Yamada was born on December 10, 1865, in the village of Takabe, Kanagawa Prefecture, now incorporated into the city of Isehara. He was the second son of a poor farmer; his mother died while he was very young and he was raised by his father Shimpei. Before completing the fourth grade he had to find work. By the time he was ten he had to leave home.

In the chapter "On Yamada Waka" in *Success Stories of Women of the Taishō Period*, the author Sawada Bushō interviewed Kakichi, who gave the following account of himself.

I had neither the time, the money nor the opportunity to study as other students did. My family sent me to apprentice in a lumber yard before I was ten, but I was virtually useless because of my size. I had to pick up the nails from the floor. That was my job. But I loved to read. When I was a little older, I walked thirteen kilometers after work to attend night school. If I stayed behind to ask the teacher questions, I would not get back until morning.

At thirteen, I walked to Tokyo, seventy-eight kilometers away, and found a job in a tinker shop. The shorter hours enabled me to study longer at night. I learned Chinese and some mathematics. Finally, at twenty, I set out for America. The day after my arrival I went out looking for work.

I washed dishes at a rooming house. Then, in succession, I found employment as a cook, farmhand, sailor and railway construction worker. Despite eighteen-hour days of hard labor, I never let a day pass without studying something. I trained myself not to fall asleep before reading a few pages. Eventually I enrolled in night classes at various universities. But I couldn't afford to stay in any one place too long and, consequently, never accumulated enough credits for a degree. Still, I had a sense of satisfaction and fulfillment, especially after I changed from law to sociology.

Many young ambitious Japanese like Kakichi had left Japan for the West Coast in search of success. But as the frontier days rapidly came to an end and jobs became scarce, they had to shift their sights. Some, particularly after the Sino-Japanese and Russo-Japanese wars, headed for Manchuria and China where their country already had vested interests. Others continued to journey to America. But without money or connections, and handicapped by language, they were compelled to work hard at manual, unskilled tasks.

There were those who started from scratch and succeeded. Morinaga Taichirō, president of Morinaga Confectionery Company, brought a Western-style cookie back to Japan. He went to America at the age of twenty-four, unable to speak any English, and worked as a cook, gardener and whatnot. Somewhere along the way, he discovered how to make a delicious cookie.

Another achiever was the revolutionary socialist Katayama Sen. After many years at manual labor, he attended and graduated from Yale. The radical ideas he took back to Japan earned him an international reputation. Before long, he found himself deeply involved in labor-management issues and in the forefront of Japan's socialist movement.

There was never any doubting Yamada Kakichi's ambition, but he was always more interested in learning than in acquiring either material or personal benefits, but it was,

The Yamadas before they returned to Japan from the
United States. They were married in 1904 or 1905.

nevertheless, a struggle. In fact, it was harder to reach the
top in academia than in the business or political worlds.
Despite all his education, this first-rate sociologist had no hope
of getting a post in an American university. His only alternative was a private school.

Kakichi coached immigrants in oral and written English,
as well as in German, French and Spanish. When requested,
he lectured on a variety of subjects, including economics, and
his specialty, sociology. No record exists of the number of
students he had, but a couple of the better known were
Yamazaki Kesaya, socialist and lawyer, and Ichikawa Tōichi,
brother of the feminist Ichikawa Fusae. Kakichi was thirty-
eight years old in 1904 when Waka was registered at his
school.

He was still single, too preoccupied to consider romantic
or family ties. His proposal to Waka and her acceptance came

as a complete but welcome surprise to those at Cameron House. Of course, Kakichi knew about the inhabitants of the settlement house.

Many years later a journalist for the woman's magazine *Shufunotomo* wrote an article based on an interview with Kakichi and Waka. Published in August, 1933, it was called "Yamada Kakichi and Waka: A Couple Wedded by the Hand of God." Kakichi was quoted as follows.

Although Waka was uneducated she was remarkably intelligent, with a fine memory and an ability to grasp subtleties. She seemed anxious to learn, anxious to be given the opportunity. I, in turn, wanted to teach her everything she requested, certain that given the chance, her natural talents would help her overcome a late start in life. I could well have afforded to give her a scholarship to my school, but I was afraid people would gossip if I offered both instruction and financial assistance. So I decided to help her and make her my wife at the same time. No one would mind, I thought.

Waka discussed her marriage in an article that appeared in October, 1934. She wrote it just after Kakichi's death and it was called "To My Husband Waiting for Me in Heaven." She said, "When I met him, I felt I was the worst kind of human being, an illiterate, nothing but a poor farmer's daughter. But Kakichi did not look at me as a lesser being. He treated me like a lady, which made me reexamine myself. Eventually, I gained self-respect."

That he treated her as an equal while fully aware of her

past enabled their relationship to deepen into one of mutual understanding. This, along with another consideration, led Waka into marriage. In the same article, she went on to say:

> He was tough, unshakable, like a rock that withstands the buffeting of powerful waves. I appreciated his strong character and also the irony behind his comments. Some people, however, reacted negatively to his sharp tongue. Sometimes it seemed to me that he was so busy learning and earning a living that he allowed his emotions to dry up. I wanted to make a home for one who had never known a mother's love.

She became a new person after her conversion—no longer self-centered, no longer capable of profiting from another's weakness, as had been the case with Tachii. In fact, she sensed that she had something worthwhile to contribute to marriage.

Rev. Sakabe, Donaldina Cameron and others at the mission house welcomed the prospect of Waka's marriage, but there was a provision: Kakichi had to agree to submit to baptism and confirmation so that the wedding could be held in church. Kakichi, an avowed atheist, refused to compromise his beliefs, not even as a formality, notwithstanding that a church wedding was very important in those days, although the marriage would have been legal if performed by a justice of the peace.

Some members of the Presbyterian Church spoke out against Kakichi as if he were the devil incarnate. He remained adamant and inflexible. In the end, the marriage took place in the church. Cameron, who put Waka's happiness above everything else, concluded that Waka would have eloped.

According to Waka, it was a simple ceremony. "After the clergyman gave us his blessing, everyone had a piece of cake and wished us well. I gathered my belongings and bid farewell. Kakichi and I then went to Bush Street where his friend Shibuya Bato had prepared coffee for the three of us."

The exact day and year of the wedding are not certain, but it must have occurred in the fall of 1904 or the spring of 1905, judging from this Cameron House newsletter by Miss E. A. Stodge in 1905: "We lost a Japanese girl to marriage. She had been working with us for some time and was perfectly suited to her job because of her past experiences and superb intelligence."

Before their marriage Kakichi and Waka erected a tombstone for Tachii Nobusaburō in the Japanese cemetery at Colma, a suburb south of San Francisco. Kakichi insisted Waka create a proper burial place and hold a memorial service.

The story of Tachii's suicide must have reached Kakichi's ears, since news like that traveled quickly in the Japanese community. Or at some point Waka herself might have revealed something about her relationship with Tachii.

The simple funeral arranged by Washizu had disturbed Kakichi perhaps because only a wooden stick marked the site.

"Really, you cannot leave his body as it is," he said. Kakichi acted out of compassion for the man who had loved Waka enough to risk his life for her. Whatever the background, Waka had a headstone made and planted several rose bushes around the stone.

Not everyone favored Kakichi's unusual marriage. Some criticized him for "marrying such a woman, her above all others." The criticism came from even his closest friends. Others laughed at him "for competing for a woman's love with a dead man." The ridicule did not bother Kakichi. He was seasoned and had learned to insulate himself against prejudices. His task, as he saw it, was to educate his wife. He spent many hours correcting her English and Japanese, and instructed her in a multitude of new fields: world history, law, economics, sociology. Sometimes his intensity and determination were too much for her.

"My husband tried to pour all his knowledge and past experience into my brain. As for me, I sometimes would have preferred cooking. If I forgot where I put my book Kakichi became furious and pulled me out of the kitchen."

There is another passage in the same vein. "When I got a little too involved in housework or behind in a reading assignment, he thundered his disapproval. 'Why must you waste your time being an ordinary housewife?' I was so frightened I returned straight to my studies."

Waka would have been content to wait on him and do household chores while he taught and earned money, but Kakichi was intent on fulfilling his original plan—to help Waka realize her potential. That was his goal; that was what would make him happy. The couple might have lived in San Francisco forever, but on April 18, 1906, at 5:13 A.M. disaster struck.

One of this centuries great earthquakes shook the city. More than half of the buildings were either destroyed or razed by raging fires. Kakichi and Waka were not spared and in the aftermath of the devastation decided to return to their homeland. Having lost several thousand books he had sweated to accumulate over the years, Kakichi was deeply saddened. But he also may have wished to start over in a community where no one knew about Waka's past. For these reasons and perhaps others, forty-one-year-old Kakichi and his wife of twenty-nine sailed from San Francisco for Yokohama. Kakichi had not seen the mountains of his youth for over twenty-one years. Waka had been away from her native village for more than nine.

The Roses of Colma

Several weeks had passed since I arrived in San Francisco, and the year was drawing to a close. One unfulfilled wish remained before I felt I could leave for home. I had to see with my own eyes where Tachii Nobusaburō was buried. Kakichi had gone to some trouble to ensure a proper burial for a man to whom he felt bound in an oddly poignant friendship because of their mutual love for Yamada Waka.

Dead people are soon forgotten even when their descendants make a habit of visiting their graves. In the case of Tachii, who had been alone in a new country, I wondered if there was anything to see after seventy years. As Kawase drove me to the cemetery at Colma, I again went over in my mind what I knew of the tragic love affair.

The Japanese cemetery at Colma goes back to the beginning of the century and is the largest eternal resting place for Japanese-Americans. The first three Japanese to die in San Francisco had been sailors on the *Kanrin-maru*, a ship that accompanied the first shogunate mission to the United States. The date was 1860 and the shogun's ambassador was Shimmi Buzen no Kami. The dead sailors were buried on Laurel Hill in the city itself. Later, as the number of Japanese coming to America increased following the Meiji Restoration, the Oriental community felt a need to have its own cemetery. After an incident in 1879 in which a young Japanese prostitute was denied burial, a sense of urgency set in, and the Japanese community acquired its own plot of land, a beautiful site overlooking San Francisco Bay. Then, in 1902, much larger grounds were purchased at Colma and all the tombstones were moved there.

It was clear and sunny at the cemetery, which seemed to be well laid out. I observed a mixture of Western style and Japanese grave markers, the latter usually flanked by two stone lanterns. The grass was neatly trimmed and there were pleasant shady groves everywhere, planted by the families of the deceased. I was told that the place had deteriorated during the war while people of Japanese ancestry were confined to so-called relocation camps. It had taken quite some effort to rid the place of the weeds and to prune the overgrown trees.

I searched for some three hours but failed to find Tachii's stone. The caretaker that day knew nothing and after a while I left.

That night I called Shimizu and several older residents of San Francisco. One of them, a Mr. Asano who was on the board of directors of the *Nichibei Jiji Shimbun,* knew the location of Tachii's tomb and offered to take me to it the next morning.

Asano was eighty but set a brisk pace through the cemetery. He headed straight for the site which was situated amid other old stones dating back three quarters of a century.

"Right over there, Yamazaki-san," he said, pointing to a square stone about three feet high set on a double pedestal. After so many years of exposure to the elements, the surface was badly pitted and cracked. The writing on the front and back of the stone was thoroughly weathered and difficult to read.

Asano wet some tissue at a nearby tap. I did the same with my handkerchief and the two of us wiped the surface of the stone until the inscription was again legible. On the front: "Tomb of Tachii Nobusaburō." On the back, three lines: "Born March 2, 1871. Died December 5, 1903. Erected by Asaba Waka."

There it was—the only memento of the man who had played the key role in the first act to the Arabian Oyae's transformation. It was also verification for all the data I had collected about Yamada.

The caretaker came by and asked about my relationship to the dead person, remarking that there had been no visitors to the tomb in the past thirty years.

"A lot of rose bushes used to surround the grave. They blossomed every spring. I never could figure out why but they all died about twenty years ago. I felt terrible."

A moment's calculation told me that the roses disappeared about the time of Yamada's death. Coincidence, of course. While I do not believe in an eternal soul or life after death, I had the strange feeling that the roses had been somehow infused with Tachii's spirit and had watched over Waka even

The author stands beside the grave of Tachii Nobusaburō in Colma, California. The inscription gives his name and the word "tomb."

when she returned to Japan. When she died, the roses also withered.

I wished I had brought some flowers from San Francisco. Tachii would have appreciated them from a person who admired Yamada. I looked around, but it was winter and there were no wild flowers. I took out my red silk handkerchief, shaped it like a rose, and placed it at the base of the stone with small pebbles around it. My final farewell.

Back in the city I said good-bye to all those who had been so kind and helpful and left for the airport. In no time we were above the clouds. As the twinkling red and blue lights of the city receded, my thoughts again turned to Tachii. I tried to see him from Yamada's point of view. Why had she failed to write a single line about the man who threw away his life for her? Not a word. All her feelings of love and appreciation went to Kakichi, her "teacher and husband." Then Ichikawa Fusae's account of that night in Nagoya came back to me, the night in which Waka had confided to her friend Hiratsuka Raichō, "I don't mind, but Daddy would be upset. So please don't tell anyone."

Yamada Kakichi had to protect both his name and that of his wife. It is quite understandable that he wanted to conceal Waka's days as an Ameyuki-san. And since Tachii was connected with those years, Waka had to keep him buried. And he remained so . . . until I came along.

There was a postscript to the foregoing at the time my account of Yamada Waka's life was serialized in the monthly *Bungei Shunjū* magazine. Right after the appearance of the Tachii episode, I received a phone call from a certain Komiyama Teruko. She explained that she had five aunts who were most anxious to find out whether this Tachii Nobusaburō had been their relative. They had such an uncle whom they fondly remembered and still spoke of although the Tachii family, feeling disgraced, virtually disowned their son. It was natural for the family to contact me, since my story showed respect and admiration for Tachii.

Komiyama took me to visit one of the aunts, Kishida Yoshiko, in the late autumn of 1977. In spite of her age, she was a strikingly beautiful and elegant woman, and she was eager to tell me what she knew about Tachii.

She said that Nobusaburō was the third child of Tachii Shin. He was born in 1871 into a distinguished Nagoya family, which had served the Tokugawa shoguns until the Meiji Restoration. Kishida knew very little about Nobusaburō's youth except that he was reputed to be intelligent. This she had learned from her mother Kim who had married Tachii Seitarō, Nobusaburō's oldest brother, at the age of sixteen.

Yoshiko then went on to describe the fate of her mother. She stated that although Kim was pretty, she did not come from a samurai family that was anywhere nearly as venerable as the Tachii clan. As a result, her mother suffered, sometimes experiencing harsh treatment from her in-laws. This was not unusual. The mother-in-law in a two- or three-generation household was a figure to be reckoned with. Despite the dissolution of feudalism and the conscious striving for modernization, feudal notions and customs did not disappear overnight.

Of all the Tachiis, Nobusaburō alone had showed kindness, affection and understanding towards her. She, in turn, cared for him as an older sister (she was four years his senior). Eventually, the age factor became less of a barrier. Kim grew more and more dependent on Nobusaburō for comfort and understanding. The details of this tender relationship are not known, but one day, without warning, Tachii suddenly left for America and was never heard from again. Some years later, word reached his parents that he had been "poisoned" by a harlot called the Arabian Oyae.

Kishida learned from her older sister that their father Seitarō cried profusely and in public at the news of his brother's death. No one knows of the bitter tears shed by his wife, although in public Kim observed the mores of her class and concealed her emotions. Her own grief remained deeply and secretly buried in her heart.

Seitarō's open expression of grief did not faze the Tachii clan. They felt Nobusaburō had dishonored the family name and refused to put his name on their altar. In fact, Nobusaburō's name was altogether obliterated from the family history. Although the years passed, Kim remembered, and through her, all the other female members of the Tachii family also remembered.

Kim spoke of Nobusaburō with much affection, referring to him in a polite way as "Nobu-sama." He had been tall, handsome, starry-eyed and tender. Kishida said she often wondered whether her mother hadn't loved him best of all.

I had no way of judging that but it seemed that in the beginning, Nobusaburō's compassion towards his beautiful sister-in-law had been motivated by a genuine desire to help her adjust to the Tachiis. His compassion no doubt turned into admiration and love. Kim's fondness for her brother-in-law must also have grown, but she probably behaved as if her obligations to the Tachiis took precedence over her personal feelings. Nobusaburō realized that he could never marry his sister-in-law even if she could have obtained a divorce. He no doubt decided that it was best to go away and thus end their mutual misery. He may have hoped that in a strange environment he would in time forget Kim. On the other hand, in the foreign land his loneliness and sense of loss may have been accentuated.

Did he head straight for the streets of Seattle? Who knows? All that is certain is that he met the Arabian Oyae, fell in love with her and risked his life for her. An oddball, a loner, he had a decisive predilection for unhappy women who suffered as outcasts.

Until the Tachii family read my story, they never questioned that their son had been murdered by the Arabian Oyae. Now, learning the truth, they felt obligated to restore Nobusaburō's good name. A memorial service was held so that his soul could finally rest in peace. Kishida Yoshiko was extremely happy to learn that her mother had loved someone worthy and expressed her intention to visit Nobusaburō's grave at Colma. She spoke the last sentence tearfully, as if she herself were suffering from the excruciating pain of a forbidden love.

Yotsuya Iga-chō

$\mathcal{I}$t was much easier to pursue Yamada Waka's life after her return with Kakichi to Japan. Hiratsuka Raichō's *Autobiography*, *Seitō* and *Woman and the New Society*, edited by Waka herself, provided excellent material. As my own articles on Yamada Waka's life unfolded in *Bungei Shunjū*, readers wrote and offered bits of information and suggestions. Through a series of coincidences, I was led to the Yamada house in Yotsuya Iga-chō, a visit I had intended to make but had not yet gotten around to.

I was writing short feature articles on some of the interesting people I met, such as the old first-generation immigrants in America. Tamesa had made a particularly strong impression on me. I had the feeling I could never repay him for his extraordinary kindness and invaluable help. I admired his independent spirit; at ninety-two he preferred to live alone rather than with his children. In one article I praised him so highly as a model for the elderly that I received numerous responses from readers, one from a woman who said that her parents had known the kind, gentle Tamesa when they had lived in Seattle many, many years ago. She added that her mother would have liked to hear more about him but because of her age was unable to go out much.

I took the hint and went to visit the old woman, feeling it was the least I could do in view of my indebtedness to Tamesa. We chatted about a number of things, and then she unexpectedly remarked that she knew a Satō Tei, a woman whose early experiences had been similar to Tamesa's. She said Satō had learned to sew from Waka's sister Yae.

Naturally, I contacted the woman immediately. The interview was informal and friendly. Satō spoke of the Yamada house in Iga-chō in the Yotsuya district, a section of the city which had not changed very much. She described the large downstairs room, decorated modestly in Western style with shelves of foreign books. Waka, she remembered, used to give piano lessons, and Kakichi used to teach foreign languages. On the second floor, Yae, a widow, instructed girls and young women in kimono making and fancy needlework.

One delightfully warm and sunny day in January, 1977, I set off to find the Yamada house. Getting off the train at Yotsuya Station, I chose my route by consulting an old map published in 1896 by the Tokyo Postal Service. Every street was clearly indicated. The Yamada house was supposed to be directly opposite the Shonenji in Iga-chō. The temple has an interesting history, which includes a story linking a famous group of undercover agents with the naming of Iga-chō. It seems that the name comes from a group of *ninja* who called themselves Iga. They had been in the service of the Tokugawa shoguns under the leadership of Hattori Honzo. When Hattori decided to abandon the adventurous life and enter the Buddhist priesthood, he took the name Shonen and built the temple bearing his name. The temple was still there.

The Yamada house was rather lovely, with a latticed front door and plants everywhere. A charcoal dealer, perhaps a descendant of the one who lent Ichikawa Fusae a room when she first came to Tokyo, lived two houses away. I walked up and down the peaceful tree-lined street and suddenly realized that I had seen it all once before. Ten years earlier, when I collaborated with my husband on a book on child education, I had come here to visit Tokunaga Yuki, the principal of the Futaba Day Care Center. She had devoted herself to opening day-care centers and nursery schools, but more than two decades passed before similar facilities were provided for the less fortunate.

Tokunaga, I recalled, had been an admirer of the new breed of women, an avid reader of *Seitō* and an acquaintance of Hiratsuka Raichō. Now it all came back to me. She had told me that Hiratsuka had lived with Okumura Hiroshi, a painter several years her junior. In 1933 Hiratsuka bore a child out of wedlock. Tokunaga, proud of the fruit of this "new type of marriage," visited Hiratsuka taking a small gift for the baby. She made a point of sending a birthday gift every year until the child graduated from elementary school.

I had almost forgotten the whole incident. That night I looked up some literature of that period and discovered that Hiratsuka had lived at 42 Iga-chō, right behind the Yamada house. How did Waka and Raichō get to be friendly? How did Waka get started writing for *Seitō*? There was still a great deal to sort out.

Seitō

*E*ven though Yotsuya in 1906 was a quiet, residential section of Tokyo, it had not been the Yamadas' intention to continue living in the city. Their hard life in the United States had left them weary of urban living and ready to return to the quiet countryside. Waka's brother invited them to his farm, but after a look at the situation, the couple despaired of making a go of it there. They had neither land nor a house nor the money to acquire either. So it was that they went back to the city and settled in at number 41 Iga-chō.

Their landlord was none other than Kakichi's brother, an enterprising man who in addition to owning rental property operated a bicycle shop in Kanda. The house behind the Yamadas, which was the abode at various times of Hiratsuka Raichō, her young lover Okumura Hiroshi and a number of other interesting characters, also belonged to him.

Hundreds of Japanese had gone abroad to study, to make money, or for a host of other reasons. Some returned to capitalize on their knowledge of the west. One fellow printed up a humorous business card that read, "Graduate of the School of Hard Knocks." Kakichi, as we know, fell back on his ability to teach and attracted students simply by hanging out a sign on his gate: "Languages Taught Here—French, English, Spanish, German." The Yamadas prospered, as did many others during the 1910s and 1920s, a comparatively liberal period that has come to be known as Taishō Democracy. It is very likely that they were able to purchase their own house and improve the property.

It was a time of tolerance, open-mindedness and international awakening. After World War I, the bourgeoisie, which had made windfall profits, showed a tendency to accept liberal ideas from abroad and even a tolerance towards the socialist writers who, having failed to overthrow the government, were reduced to theorizing in the new journals. Unusual private

The cover of *Seitō*, a women's magazine, issue of November, 1911. *Seitō* is a direct translation of "Bluestocking," an 18th century English women's literary club.

schools like Kakichi's were also popular. At some point, one can assume that for some it became fashionable to attend the Yamada Language School, or whatever it was called. Other men and women, infatuated with languages and foreign cultures, attended in earnest. The Yamadas' house was filled with all kinds of people: white collar workers studying English for professional reasons, high school and college students and those motivated by a passionate intellectual curiosity. The non-affluent fell into this latter category. Kakichi preferred this last group to the others and soon assembled a small coterie that became the core of an old-fashioned salon.

Among those who belonged to this inner circle was Ōsugi Sakae. He was the leader of Japan's anarchists after Kōtoku Shūsui was put to death for trying to assassinate the emperor. While most of Ōsugi's friends were implicated in this seditious conspiracy and were arrested, Ōsugi survived simply because he had been in jail for another offense when the plan was concocted. Ōsugi was in and out of jail quite often and between convictions he studied languages and literature at Kakichi's. It was said that he mastered one foreign language after each imprisonment. Another undertaking, together with fellow socialist Arahata Kanson, was the founding of the magazine called "Modern Thought."

Kakichi loved to teach. To a large extent it was his desire to educate Waka that induced him to marry her. He believed that she showed great promise and continued to be her mentor; he encouraged her to become an expert and to express herself on issues concerning women—his own area of expertise. With the aid of Ōsugi, he succeeded in getting Waka admitted to the Seitō Society.

Ōsugi sent Hiratsuka Raichō the manuscript of Waka's first translations, along with a letter of introduction. Although Hiratsuka was not personally acquainted with Ōsugi, she knew of his reputation and scrutinized Waka's works very carefully. Waka had translated difficult essays by a leading female liberationist of that time, the South African Olive Shriner. Finding the work to be excellent prose, poetic in tone, accurate and good reading, Hiratsuka published it in the November, 1914, issue of *Seitō*.

Not long afterward Hiratsuka received a letter from Kakichi requesting an interview. After the meeting at the *Seitō* office, Hiratsuka described the Yamadas. Of Kakichi she said, "He is straightforward and sincere, rather serious, too. He is past fifty, tall, well built and evidently older than his wife. It struck me that he had trouble with some Japanese idioms, perhaps because of his long sojourn in America." She added that although this was their first encounter, Kakichi proceeded to speak of very personal matters. He related how he met his wife, their mutual love and decision to return to Japan, and their current undertakings. He spelled out his expectations for Waka and managed somehow to ask that she be admitted into the Seitō Society.

"Mrs. Yamada listened quietly until her husband finished and then spoke in a manner that was humble but at the same time did not conceal a deep sense of self-confidence. She said 'I was not educated until very late because I had to go to work as a child. I'm not sure I'll be able to keep up with the rest of you.'"

Hiratsuka commented later, "Her good nature was apparent from the start and I remember being charmed by her, although she was older than myself, dressed plainly, and was as big as an elephant."

Towards the end of 1914 the Seitōsha decided to change the focus of their magazine. Their new goal was to raise the level of women's consciousness about their role in society and to help women cultivate individual talents so that they could become more productive members of society. *Seitō* at this point was in the hands of its new editor, Itō Noe, who agreed with the activist thrust. *Seitō*'s pages were open to "any woman writer who loves literature and accepts the group's purpose." To be admitted one had to submit a curriculum vitae along with a short essay explaining reasons for applying and ten pages of an article which could be poetry, translation or creative fiction. The shift in emphasis away from the purely literary favored Waka, who was already quite involved and knowledgeable about issues confronting women.

Waka introduced Hiratsuka and other Seitōsha members to Kakichi and soon all of them wanted to audit his class on the Swedish author Ellen Kaye. Itō Noe, Saiga Kinko, Okada Yuki, Ichikawa Fusae, the well-known writer Yoshiya Nobuko—soon it seemed as if Kakichi were giving private lectures just for the women of Seitōsha.

The Yamadas were exceedingly kind to their students, taking care of them outside as well as inside the classroom. Itō Noe, for instance, who was thoroughly in despair because of marital difficulties with her second husband, Tsuji Jun, would not have weathered the storms in her life without the steady support and guidance of the Yamadas. Even Hiratsuka came to depend on them. When she wanted to continue her studies during pregnancy, the Yamadas encouraged

Prominent women (1934): (from left) Yosano Akiko, Okamoto Kanoko, Hagi Ayako, Kamichika Ichiko, Fukao Tsumako, Yamada Waka and Ikuta Hanayo.

her to move nearby so that she would not have to commute, which is how she and her mate came to inhabit number 42 Iga-chō.

A long list of occupants, some rather odd, had lived there. Before Hiratsuka there was the eccentric socialist lawyer Yamazaki Kesaya, who insisted on posing in the nude for a photograph in "Who's Who in Law." His colleagues next to him were clothed in formal kimono. Then there was Hori Yasuko, who depended on the Yamadas for many many years after Ōsugi left her for Itō Noe. Jealousy nearly killed her but she managed to hang on. She was bedridden, but nonetheless outlived Ōsugi and Itō by almost a year, thanks to the kind advice of the Yamadas.

By that time, Waka was writing and translating at a prolific rate. After Olive Shriner, in whom she sensed a kindred spirit, she moved to the works of Lester Ward, an American botanist and sociologist whose specialty was women's education, and then to Ellen Kaye. She also wrote two original short stories, "Primroses" and "Tora-san." In issue after issue of _Seitō_, articles by Waka on a wide range of subjects were sure to appear. She expressed her views on such subjects as abortion, free love, natural instinct and education. _Seitō_ was dismissed by some as a radical and imitative magazine (imitative of Europe's _Bluestocking_, the organ for the "new women" seeking voting rights), but journalists could not ignore it. They were quick to pounce on the "new women" and often falsely accused them of looseness and immorality. Still the women remained in the limelight.

The general public, it should be noted, warmly supported women's causes, but did not take _Seitō_ or its contributors seriously. Perhaps the magazine was a bit too progressive for even the educated public.

Waka, because of her originality and prolificacy, cast the Seitōsha in a new perspective. Many of the subjects she covered in her articles were topics that Kakichi had lectured on. He was the expert on women and prided himself on his understanding, but he was even more eager to impart his ideas to Waka. Throughout the 1910s and 1920s Kakichi remained the invisible force behind the women's movement, and he was treated with great respect.

Kakichi's favorite subject to lecture on was Lester Ward. Waka absorbed everything and subsequently made a compilation of Kakichi's lectures to which she added her own translations. She published Ward's *Scientific Attitudes toward Women, Women's Natural Instincts, Women's Education,* and Ellen Kaye's books, *Love and Marriage* and *A Century for Children.* The masses of women were beginning to think about issues concerning them, and Waka stood out as an invaluable social critic. From 1914 to 1916 she published continuously in *Seitō.* When Itō Noe took over, she made sure that *Seitō* was transformed from a purely literary journal into a full-fledged women's liberation journal.

In September, 1916, *Seitō* was published for the last time. Its ideals were later revived by Hiratsuka Raichō and Ichikawa Fusae, who in 1920 as noted earlier, organized the New Women's Association.

One by one the Seitō women either married or formed marital arrangements. Faced with the daily concerns of ordinary women—shopping, children, budgeting—they needed the Yamada's guidance even more than before. From the Yamadas, Hiratsuka Raichō and her mate learned to live simply and frugally. Hiratsuka reported that Kakichi smoked the cheapest cigars and that when Waka went shopping she bought the daily specials, and never anything beyond a certain price. Waka, she said, used to call to her out the window to turn off the lights and stop wasting electricity. Their one luxury was books. She said the Yamadas had a magnificent library of foreign literature which they bought from the Maruzen Book Store.

The Yamadas advised newlyweds on practical, down-to-earth matters and helped them adjust to their new family roles and responsibilities. The seminars at Kakichi's continued, but on this practical level. Liberation was still an important subject but it was discussed within a new framework of probability. It was no longer fashionable to be a radical romantic. The *Seitō* flowers blossomed now into different and distinct petals. Some began to advocate the protection of motherhood, others became suffragettes. (Women had no voting rights and did not gain them until after World War II.) Some joined the socialist women's movement.

Waka joined the New Women's Association but did not participate fully. Instead she started a magazine, "Women and the New Society," for which she wrote essays and commentaries on the times. She also began to write for other newspapers and magazines. It should be noted that she was a writer and not an activist. In 1920 her collected essays were published. Included were "Love and Society," "Society and the Family," "Women Bow Down to Society," and an article on prostitutes. The following year with her translation of Magdalene Marx's *Women*, her stature as a female critic became solidly established. Despite her reputation as a writer-translator, she was known only to a few intellectuals, those who read the culture sections of newspapers and magazines. This was in part due to her subject matter and heavy style.

The educated did look to her for ideas. In "Women Bow Down to Society," she discussed labor unions, working conditions for girls at the loom, volunteer workers, voting rights, Hull House, the New Women's Association and new trends in women's thinking. By the beginning of the Showa period (1926), Yamada Waka's popularity extended to the masses, and her name became known all over Japan.

This occurred as a result of her being selected by the *Tokyo Asahi Shimbun* as the woman to write their Advice to Women column. The prototype for this type of column had already appeared in 1880 in *Kojun* magazine. More and more journals and newspapers published these personal advice columns. Readers often asked bizarre questions and accented the sensual beyond what could have been considered good taste and common sense. But since the questions were authentic, their impact was all the more powerful and newspapers came to use this column as a means of increasing their circulation. The *Asahi* did not join the herd until May 1, 1931, when they were forced to swallow their pride and inaugurate such a column. They chose Waka and another woman; the latter quit after three months and Waka handled it by herself. The *Asahi* soon increased its circulation to two million.

Kakichi stood proudly by, in the background but basking in his wife's accomplishments. He continued his own studies and the accumulation of knowledge in the social sciences. For him, it was enough to watch his wife expound his theories and comment on issues which he had discussed with her. Why did he refuse center stage? One reason may be that his writing in Japanese was not very good. Hiratsuka pointed out that his speech was awkward, and it is possible that his writing was still worse. In his entire lifetime he had published only two books, one on Western cuisine (1904) and the other, an introduction to sociology. The cookbook had had a coauthor.

Perhaps a more important reason was that Kakichi was a devotee of Lester Ward (1841–1913), a scientist who did much to transform sociology into an academic discipline. He was the first president of the American Sociological Society (1906–7) and wrote a great deal. His book *Pure and Ap-*

plied Sociology, which has as its subtitle *On the Origin of the Spontaneous Development of Society*, had as its thesis the general supremacy of the female of the species in society. Ward pointed out that in the course of history the matriarchy was replaced by male dominance. Men subjugated women, causing them to regress. Women were forced to fall back on their biological functions while men had the opportunity to develop their brains. Ward theorized that women would eventually bounce back and that equality between the sexes would be restored. Kakichi tried to practice Ward's ideas in his own marriage. For intellectual as well as emotional reasons he wanted Waka to succeed. In fact, it gave him a vicarious thrill and sense of satisfaction to watch her express the ideas and thoughts which he had formulated or developed. Waka thoroughly understood her husband's intentions and desires. She dedicated her first book, "Love and Society," "To my husband who taught me the ABCs, how to read and write. If my work is of any value, it is the result of his efforts."

Few men (then or now) can feel and behave the way Kakichi did when confronted by their wives' success. Frustration and jealousy is the rule. The camaraderie and deep respect that governed Kakichi's and Waka's lives was, and is still, the exception. There was an example of this within their own circle in the person of Tsuji Jun, who could not stand Itō Noe's popularity as an editor. He insisted on a divorce and went on to live a very bohemian life.

A Very
Maternal Woman

*Y*amada Waka's great achieve-
ment was in reaching the masses through her simplicity and
honesty and gaining their trust and respect. Notwithstanding her husband's contributions, Waka's success must be
credited to her alone. In the final analysis, it was her own
past experiences that formed her unique way of thinking and
led her to support, first, the idea of female economic independence, and then the concept of maternalism.

Yamada's past was a constant reminder that an uneducated
woman will be forever doomed to the sort of indignities she
suffered. She wanted women to be schooled, to have a trade
or profession, and to be able to participate in their society,
and she encouraged women to find work that paid an honest
wage: work on farms, in factories, offices—domestic labor,
such as that performed by the ordinary housewife, was ob-
viously excluded.

Her preoccupation with liberation through work is reflected
in her early translations of Olive Shriner, particularly "Three

Dreams," in which a woman gets the chance to work as a result of the invention of a machine. In those days, Yamada admired the Industrial Revolution and the capitalist system, which gave women the opportunity to work. Only later, as she came to stand for—literally embody—the concept of maternalism, did she begin to criticize democracies for their rugged individualism.

While writing for the *Asahi*, Waka developed her ideas on maternalism, ideas whose strength, in must be admitted, did not lie in their originality.

As early as 1915, Hiratsuka Raichō became embroiled with Yosano Akiko, a famous poet and writer, in a public dispute over the important issues confronting women. One of them was the issue of maternalism. Yosano, urging complete economic independence for women, was against giving them any special protection for being mothers. As she put it, "I am against according women financial assistance and government protection before and after childbirth. Just as it is a form of slavery for women to depend on men in exchange for performing sexual services, it is equally undesirable for women to accept any form of aid from the state. Women must liberate themselves from all outside forces. To do so requires a good education, determination and the will to work."

Although not disputing the importance of economic independence for women, Hiratsuka argued that, in addition, a woman had the right to demand protection as a mother. She reasoned that a woman simply by fulfilling her duty to society by bearing children had the right to demand that society protect her afterwards. Nor should such protection demean a woman. On the contrary, a woman should be made to feel as if hers was a privileged status. Only then would she be freed from the terrible conflict of having to choose between raising a family and learning a profession. She further asserted that the state and the private sectors of society ought to share the burden of helping women to become mothers.

The debate between Hiratsuka and Yosano seesawed back and forth. Hiratsuka, nourished on Ellen Kaye's work "The Renaissance of Maternity" and Kakichi's lectures on the subject, was annoyed with her colleague's lack of understanding and compassion. Eventually, other women were drawn into the arena. One was a socialist. Yamakawa Kikue criticized both women. According to her the solution to the question of maternity as well as other issues confronting women depended on the abolition of the capitalist system. She accused Yosano of a bourgeois mentality and Hiratsuka of being a compromising revisionist.

Yamada entered the fray by writing in defense of maternal protection. By today's standards, and certainly by those of her own time, she held rather traditional views on maternity. She abandoned her earlier emphasis on work. Like Hiratsuka, she was influenced by Ellen Kaye but she differed from her friend in one respect. She maintained that only "exceptionally talented women" should go to work, that "most women should stay home and create the proper environment for their husbands and children," that "children grow up healthier if they have a mother's nurturing," and that "a husband finds strength and energy in a home that is cared for by a loving wife." In other words, "a happy home life should be a woman's first concern, not the production of goods."

A portrait of Yamada Waka from the period 1912–16, when she was a regular contributor to *Seitō* magazine.

She stated that a woman employed in an office or factory is merely fulfilling a personal obligation, but in raising a child, she has the right to ask all of society to help her. And the state ought to come to her aid, particularly if her husband is unable to support her and the children. Over the years she consistently and forcefully spoke out in defense of maternalism, although her reasoning was not as sophisticated as Hiratsuka's. The lack of originality, sophistication and her heavy style were perhaps reasons why many of the books on women's liberation omit Yamada Waka's contributions when referring to the dispute on maternalism.

Unlike Hiratsuka, Yosano and the others, Yamada deserves

a special place. Her principles were not formulated in the abstract. She lived, or tried to live, according to what she preached by extending a helping hand to all who came to her. The Yamada house became a refuge for the needy.

I interviewed several people who had known her: Hanafusa Haruko, a long-time neighbor; Ikeda Fumio, a student who obtained free room and board from the Yamadas; Kojima Yasue, whom Kakichi taught Western cooking; Mukai Eiko, a dentist who worked with Waka in community activities in Yotsuya; Takebe Ritsu, dorm mother at the Hatagaya House for Mothers and Children. All without exception testified to Waka's extraordinary generosity, strength and kindness.

One story in particular, told by Morita Toyoko, illustrates the nature of Yamada's maternalism. Morita, born in 1912 and now headmistress of a nursing school in Tokyo, told me that "Yamada Waka was my benefactress. But to help you understand what a wonderful person she was, I will have to reveal my shameful past.

"I was born," she said, "Into a pawnbroker's family on Shikoku Island and at twenty married into a rich farmer's family. My husband, a spoiled creature, was engaged in the family business, distributing oranges in Kobe, but he started to drink and run after other women soon after our marriage. He was out late three or four nights a week and came home drunk. When he ran out of money, he went to his parents and begged for more. I began to hate him so bitterly that if he came near me I felt like a prostitute. When I could no longer stand the idea of selling my body to a man I didn't care for, I thought about a divorce. I spent several sleepless nights, then I left him. I left behind my year-old daughter as well. This happened when I was twenty-two years old."

Unable to go back to her own folks because they would have sent her straight back to Kobe, she headed for Tokyo. From the train station she went to the offices of *Shufunotomo* to get the Yamadas' address, since Waka was a regular contributor to the magazine.

"You can understand why I wanted to see her. Besides, I remembered the time she came to lecture at our high school. Her words stuck with me. 'A woman,' she said, 'does not have to put up with cruelty just because she's a woman.' She also said, 'men and women are equal' and 'one should not buy rice from a store whose owner keeps a mistress.' She told us that 'a woman has the right to hit a delivery man if he assaults her sexually.' "

From *Shufunotomo* she went to the Yamadas' house. Waka was sick in bed that day, but Kakichi was kind to her. He listened to her tale of woe and later presented Morita to his wife, saying, "This woman has come all the way up here to see you. I suggest she stay with us for a while."

Waka wrote to Morita's parents and husband and both her father and husband came to Tokyo. Her father quickly gave up trying to persuade her to go back to her husband. Even so, her husband won out. He had only to mention that "the child is crying for her day and night" and she gave in.

"The thought of my child in distress was more than I could bear," Morita told me. "I went back to my husband for her sake. As I put on my shoes and said good-bye, Waka whispered, 'Toyo-san, if you have to leave again, be sure to come here and nowhere else.'

"She touched me deeply. What a relief it was to know that

if I were pushed to the brink, there was somewhere for me to go, someone who cared."

Her husband's lifestyle did not change. The marriage was soon headed for disaster. At the age of twenty-six, Morita finally summoned up the courage to leave again, this time with her child. She went directly to the Yamadas.

"Waka's bosom was like a shelter for battered wives," she said. Again her husband came to Tokyo, but she was determined to resist his overtures despite his threats to take the child away from her. By law, he claimed, the child belonged to his family.

"Can you imagine the dilemma of having to choose between giving up my flesh and blood or living with a despicable husband?" she asked. "I wrestled with my conscience and decided to be firm."

That night her husband took away her child. Her grief was uncontrollable. Tears flooding her cheeks, she felt the ache of a broken heart.

Waka held her close and tried to comfort her. "Cry Toyo-san," she advised. "Cry if it will help." She understood the grief of a mother without ever having been one herself. Her understanding and compassion helped Morita to find the strength to continue living.

"I was not the only person Waka rescued," she added. "She was kind to all the underdogs, especially women and children. I personally witnessed her extraordinary kindness during my long stay with the Yamadas."

When she arrived, there were already fourteen others, some of them relatives, living under the same roof. There was Tamio and his wife Koma. Tamio was Waka's nephew, adopted as a child. It was said that his real mother worked as a nurse in some hospital and died before Tamio was ten. Koma, Kakichi's niece, had been brought to the Yamadas to receive an education. Later, Tamio and Koma married and bore a son, Kunihisa. He was four when Morita went to live with the Yamadas.

There was another young child in the house. Shin had come all the way across the ocean from America at the age of six. His story made the newspapers under the headline, "Child Travels Alone From America." Shin's father, a good friend of Kakichi's, was dying of tuberculosis and wanted to save his son. When he eventually returned to Japan, he was carried by stretcher from the boat to the Yamadas. Despite the excellent care he received, he died, as did his son a few years later.

Waka's sisters Yae and Hisa occupied the house behind the Yamadas. Hisa was a typist, who married a widower with several children and raised his children, even after her husband died.

The men living with the Yamadas were all students. The Yamadas gave them free room and board and may even have paid their tuition. Each of them became quite successful. The women on the other hand, came to the Yamadas because of personal difficulties.

"The situation of Okada Fuyuko, a bright young student at the Imperial College for Women, was rather special. Her father, a fisherman in a small village on Shikoku, accidentally killed another man, bringing down the wrath of the villagers. His daughter Fuyuko was then regarded as the child of a murderer. The sensitive, unhappy Fuyuko wanted to commit suicide but went to Tokyo instead—to see Yamada Waka, of course."

Morita could not recall exactly how many borders there had been over the years. She herself stayed eight years. At the time the Yamada Language School was not operating and Waka seemed to bear the full burden of household expenses. Yet she never asked any of the borders to take on outside employment or even to do housework.

"Occasionally I offered to sew. She made sure we received a good education and training at some vocation. I was sent to a nursing school. Whenever I expressed my gratitude to her she dismissed it with 'Don't mention it. You are like one of us.' She was never patronizing, which is why we were able to stay and accept her generosity.

"Her cheerfulness never ceased to amaze me. In all those years I don't recall a grouchy word or an unpleasant meal. Even in the early morning she greeted us pleasantly. I guess she was the only person in the world who could have cured the wounds that cut into my being."

Morita Toyoko's tale gives some idea of Waka's almost saintly character. Others I spoke to described similar incidents. It was clear that Yamada Waka's greatness lay more in her personality and character than in her writings. Her dedication to helping the cause of women was remembered with affection and respect twenty years after her death. Indeed she had been the perfect mother.

In the late 1930s, mothers finally came under the shelter of the law. Yamada Waka led the movement that culminated in this victory. The Depression that visibly shook up the world in 1929 had already begun to affect Japan. With the scarcity of food, family suicides increased; it was an almost daily occurrence to read about mother-child suicides. Long-time female activists who were fighting for the right to vote also organized the Motherhood Protection League. Waka was unanimously elected chairman and devoted herself to this cause. Upon Kakichi's death (in 1934 at the age of sixty-nine) Waka gave the league the substantial sum of 500 yen (about $250). Her grief was immeasurable and for a while she felt completely lost. In time, she got back on course and involved herself in women's problems.

The league petitioned both houses of the National Diet to pass a bill to protect mothers. The group also held meetings and succeeded in having their case heard. Finally, the home minister introduced a motherhood protection law to the Diet and this was enacted on March 20, 1937, two and a half years after Waka became chairman.

Yamada then launched a program to build a house for mothers and children and a nursery school. This project too came to fruition. Located in the Shibuya area of Tokyo, they were named the Hatagaya House for Mothers and Children and the Hatagaya Nursery School.

In April, 1938, Yamada rented half an acre of land from the Tokyo Municipal Office and had construction begin on the fifteen rooms for mothers and children and the nursery school to accommodate fifty children. The buildings were completed in March, 1939. Her method for raising funds was unique. She organized volunteers who were to collect used goods. This naturally infuriated men who did this kind of thing for a living, but Waka came to an agreement with them. In the end, even these men were convinced of the importance of building a house for mothers and children.

Hiratsuka Raichō and others wrote more eloquently than Yamada Waka about the importance of protecting mothers. But neither she nor her friends went as far as Yamada in doing something about it. No one except Yamada actually established a shelter, and as a columnist for the *Asahi*, she succeeded in helping thousands of women in despair.

Rape
and
Pregnancy

*L*ike many sociologists of that period, Yamada Waka believed the family constituted the backbone of a healthy society. When it became apparent to her that American-style individualism would bring no benefits to society's weaker members, namely mothers and children, she took to advocating cooperation between all the segments of society as a way of building a strong folk culture. Her conservative views on maternalism arose from this framework.

Consider this letter that appeared in the *Asahi* of March 30, 1932.

Dear Ms. Yamada:

I am turning to you because I have no one else.

I love T. He is so sweet, understanding and manly. My parents and relatives respect him. I, too, am very proud of him. He is expected to graduate from Tokyo Imperial University next spring. Now I must tell you of the horrible situation I have to face.

Last fall my father was very ill. After taking care of him for three days and spending three sleepless nights, I was exhausted and fell dead asleep the moment I hit the bed. That night a burglar broke into my room, stole my valuable watch and ring, and took something I cherish as dearly as my life—my virginity. How careless of me to have permitted this to happen! But no amount of tears or regrets can reverse my misfortune. After the incident I told my mother, and then confided in T. His reaction was most compassionate. He embraced me and said, 'Although you did not lose your chastity to me, I love you just the same.' In the days that followed he seemed more tender and understanding than before. Now I have found that I'm pregnant, and I cannot summon the courage to tell T. As kind as he is, I know he will be miserable. I feel sorry for him too. But what am I to do with this unborn child who in no way was responsible for the accident? At this moment I feel no real attachment to it, but I do feel responsible for it. So I'm torn between the child and T. At present he is away in Kyushu but due back in Tokyo early in April. He writes to me all the time and with every letter I burst into tears. Please tell me what to do.

K

Had this letter been written after World War II, the reply would have been cut and dried. A 1948 law permits abortion "in all cases where a woman is impregnated through violence, threat or rape, and cannot fight back or refuse." After 1948 abortions became commonplace and almost

everyone accepted them. In 1932 abortion was absolutely forbidden by law under all circumstances, even as a result of
rape. Yamada's astonishing reply in her column "Love for
Humanity" must be judged against the social climate of the
early 1930s. She wrote:

> How truly unfortunate your accident was. But regrets will
> get you nowhere. We must deal with the urgent issue before
> you, your attitude towards the unborn baby. I urge you
> to believe me when I say that from the time of conception
> you alone are responsible for your offspring. I realize that
> in our society a woman is no more than a field upon which
> a man casts his seed and that it is the male who deter-
> mines a child's lineage. I am very sorry you must bear a
> stranger's child. But that is exactly what you must do. For
> it is you, and only you, who is fully in charge of the disposi-
> tion of the child growing within you. It is *your* child, an
> extension of your own self, *your* flesh, *your* bones. It doesn't
> matter at all how you conceived. It is your child and I
> repeat, your responsibility. Think no more of the father.
> Look at it this way. You are supposed to love your
> neighbor as yourself, care for your neighbor's children as
> you would your own. These are humanitarian ideals. The
> child within you is certainly your own and that should
> make it easier. Moreover, for the good of our society, it
> is important to raise children who are loved.
> I'm sorry for T. But nothing can be changed. Besides,
> from what you say about him, I am sure that once you
> decide to raise the child to become a respectable citizen,
> T. will abide by your decision and help you.

Yamada firmly insisted that the humanitarian solution would be to bring the child into the world even if it had been conceived through rape. Because of her bluntness and sincerity, her reasoning was probably accepted. In any case, it is a matter of record that more and more readers came to trust her judgement. The *Asahi* compiled her question-and-answer columns in two volumes, publishing them under the titles "Counseling Women" (1932) and "On Love" (1936). The problems took many forms.

A prostitute wondered what she should do with a serious marriage proposal from a fine man. "Given my background," wrote the woman, "I'm afraid of spoiling his future. Yet it is very hard to give him up. I've tried several times. Please tell me what to do."

Yamada's reply: "Appreciate your good fortune and consider building your life with this nice man who loves you in spite of your unfortunate past. Think positively about a bright future with him."

Another woman married the second son of a geisha house proprietor on the condition that he never enter his father's business. The man agreed and the couple had two children. A few years later, the husband reneged and decided to go into the geisha house business to support his family more comfortably.

Yamada's advice to the wife was, "Divorce in this case might not be a bad idea. Although it will be hard to break up a family, it might be better to do so rather than risk being involved in a business that is a source of vice and tragedy. Fight against vice. Fight like a soldier for human decency."

Another woman committed adultery with a man nine years

her junior, became pregnant, and did not tell anyone, including the father, who sired the child. Her husband contracted a fatal illness. After his death, the widow wanted to marry her young lover but encountered opposition from his relatives and friends. The desperate couple contemplated suicide, hoping for a reunion in heaven.

Yamada advised the woman not to take the cowardly way out. Suicide was not the way to escape from the guilt the woman and her lover must share. She told her to marry and raise a happy child. In repentance for her adultery, she urged the woman to donate everything she had inherited from her husband to a charitable cause.

On the whole Yamada Waka's counsel shows the influence of America, her own past and her conversion to Christianity, all of which contributed to her moral positions. The years at Cameron House were forever with her. Whether the reader of today agrees with her opinions is irrelevant. What is significant is that she bucked public opinion, rejected the norms, even the trend of the times and consistently spoke out for morality.

In the rape case, her reply caused an uproar. Her extremely conservative, textbook self-righteousness shocked many of her faithful readers. The *Asahi* anticipated the commotion and set aside a whole page to discuss this controversial issue. The headline read, "Misfortune in the Life of a Woman: A Rape Case," and the subhead, "Woman Conceives of Child as Result of Rape."

Six panelists were asked to comment on the case. Their opinions divided equally into two opposing camps. One advocate of abortion wrote as follows.

As soon as the woman learned of her pregnancy it would have been natural for her to seek a doctor and have an abortion. If later she were punished by law, she would not have been dishonored. Indeed, if she were punished, the law itself ought then to be reexamined and abolished. The present law dishonors our judicial system. As to whether the young man should or should not forgive her depends on him—how much he truly loves the woman and what kind of character he has. There are men I know who marry former prostitutes.

If it is too late for an abortion, in my opinion her family ought to care for the child. Rape, like any other tragic accident and uncontrollable misfortune, must be accepted by all members of the family. They have an obligation to lessen the burden of the unhappy woman.

In the present case I advise the woman to find a doctor who will perform the abortion before it is too late.

To this, the opposition replied:

The unborn child had nothing to do with the manner of its conception. Therefore it is up to the mother to raise the child and keep in mind its best interests." Or they took the position that "a mother's instinct is so strong that I am sure that as soon as the baby is born she will do the proper thing.

There was an interesting juristic point of view which did not condone abortion, but hinted there might be "extenuating circumstances."

In this case [wrote a panelist] life has already begun in the womb. According to law an abortion is not permissible unless the mother's life is in danger. Sometimes, however, there are extenuating circumstances. But in general abortion is to be avoided. Nor is it advisable to change the current law since it would surely be abused. I urge the woman to tell her fiance immediately. Since he forgave her once, it is logical that he will do so again, pregnant or not. And if he cannot forgive her, he should have said so in the first place.

Raising the child is a separate subject. In the event it cannot be arranged for within the family, some other measure should be taken.

Pros and cons on abortion continued to be heard. A month or two later, the Tokyo Theater staged a melodrama based on the case. One critic gave the following account.

A girl falls fast asleep, dead tired, after having cared for her sick father for several days and nights. Along comes a burglar and rapes her while she's asleep. She reveals the incident to her mother and fiance. The latter shows understanding and forgiveness but then the girl discovers she's pregnant and the real tragedy begins.

Suddenly the girl tells her parents she no longer wants to marry. The distressed father finds out the reason and feels responsible for his daughter's misfortune. He tells the young man everything and begs him to marry his daughter. The young man agrees. He not only accepts the disgrace but tells everyone that he is the father. Then his brother and sister-in-law create a fuss by opposing the marriage, insisting that no man could be expected to raise or love the child of a burglar. They suggest an abortion. Eavesdropping on this conversation is the young woman herself, who immediately thinks of freeing her fiance by committing suicide. In the end, she is persuaded to go ahead with the marriage. Eighteen years go by.

The child grows up to be something of a juvenile delinquent. He wonders why his grandparents treat him coldly and one night he learns that he is the son of a thief. The poor fellow breaks down in tears, blames his mother for giving birth to him, curses all women, and prepares to leave home. His mother, overcome with temporary insanity, stabs him to death with a knife.

Whereupon the curtain abruptly falls.

Of course, the sensational drama countermanded Waka's opinions. The point was clear enough: unless abortion is contemplated in certain rape cases, the future of both offspring and parents will be tragic.

Yamada Waka remained true to her beliefs, however. Her opinions were to some extent a result of her conversion but also harmonized with her nature. Underlying it all was her desire for motherhood. Knowing that she could never bear a child created a deep vacuum and she came to regard any child as a treasure. Her advice, then, was an expression of her bottomless sorrow, the cry of a mother who could never bear a child, the cry of a woman who adored motherhood.

A
Lecture Tour of
the U.S.

$\mathcal{K}$akichi was extremely proud of his wife's transformation from lowly prostitute to popular social critic. At the same time, he knew that she must never reveal her past.

The Japanese were no different from other peoples and held women of the night in contempt. Once a girl was labeled prostitute, she would be segregated and handicapped. Marriage and a respectable job would be beyond her reach. I recall one happily married woman whose premarital jobs in a cabaret and a massage parlor caused her to be treated most harshly by her in-laws once they uncovered her past. The cold shoulder treatment could eventually drive a woman from her home, perhaps back to the streets or even to suicide. Such things happened all the time.

To protect his wife from a similar fate, Kakichi insisted that she hide her past for her own protection. Waka promised him that she would. Very few people learned about her Seattle days. To the general public, Waka and Kakichi were highly regarded intellectuals who had lived abroad. As we noted, this was the period of Taishō Democracy, and the Japanese admired Western culture, a factor which played a role in establishing Waka's credentials as a critic. Once her position was established, she had no difficulty maintaining it. No one would question her about her past. And when Waka had to refer to the United States, to admit that she had hit "rock bottom" there, people thought she meant poverty.

In her writings, there were never any real clues. She used metaphors, such as, "for several years I remained ignorant and lived a wormlike existence, a victim of man's cruelty, tossed about on a small ship," to convey a vague atmosphere of despair, but there were no direct references to people or events she had encountered.

Did Yamada mind having to clothe her background in these allusions? It is difficult to know how she felt. I did, however, hear about one interesting episode that occurred on her return to the United States.

It was the late autumn of 1937. Yamada had been writing almost exclusively for *Shufunotomo* for the past several years and the president of the magazine wanted her to give some talks in American cities to promote good will between Americans and Japanese-Americans. Waka accepted, and according to her "Correspondence from the United States," she left Yokohama on October 14 on the *Tatsuta-maru*. She arrived in San Francisco on October 28. What an emotional experience it must have been! Just forty years earlier she had left the same port, crossed the same ocean, and ended up in a brothel.

Her schedule was a busy one right from the evening of her arrival: discussions with representatives of the Japan Association in America, meetings with women from American organizations, and so on. Yet, within two days she managed to make a visit to 920 Sacramento Street. Cameron House still stood there. She wrote about it in the second of her articles in *Shufunotomo.*

"In the late afternoon of October 30, I went to see Donaldina Cameron on Sacramento Street. Never could I forget how wonderful she had been to me. Mrs. Fujita took me there, warning me to be careful of the Chinese. She said that Japanese do not usually go into Chinatown nowadays. Unfortunately, Ms. Cameron was not in. And Mrs. Fujita was right. The Chinese did stare at us. But no harm came of it."

The Chinese hostility toward the Japanese stemmed from the Japanese invasion of China in July, 1937. As the situation in their homeland worsened, Chinese hatred of the Japanese intensified.

This was apparently Yamada's only attempt to visit Cameron House. It is clear that she did not make an appointment beforehand, nor is it likely that she had carried on any correspondence with Donaldina Cameron. Heeding Kakichi's warning, Waka probably disassociated herself from her past completely. But then, three years after Kakichi's death, she may have been overwhelmed by a feeling of nostalgia and gratitude and set aside a moment to see her benefactress. But then she had no time, or did not set aside the time, to try again.

One cannot help speculating on Cameron's reactions had

she seen Waka after thirty years. Would she have recognized Asaba Waka in the fifty-seven-year-old woman dressed in a conservative Japanese kimono? Even if she had not recognized her, would she not have been pleased to learn how one girl she had rescued had turned out to be a writer and effective advocate for the motherhood protection act?

Waka lectured all over California, visiting San Jose, Maryville, Stockton and then Sacramento. More than a month was given over to this part of the trip. On December 9, she left for the East Coast, where she met members of Congress and was invited by Eleanor Roosevelt to the White House. On her return to the West Coast, her last stop was Seattle.

Motoda Kiyoko remembered Waka's talk in Seattle and told me about it.

"I'm seventy-six years old," she said. "I came to the United States in the middle twenties. I don't know anything about Waka's days in Seattle when people looked on her with disdain. But I'll never forget the day she came back here. After forty years, I can't forget it."

Only a few months had passed since the Japanese invasion of China. Americans sympathized with the Chinese and boycotted Japanese goods. Some of the Japanese were made to feel like outcasts.

"My husband and I were young and full of spirit. We owned the noodle restaurant on 5th and Main Street. We built it up into a good business. The boycott didn't affect us too much. You don't know, Yamazaki-san, how hard it is to have your own business in this country."

She said she and her husband were childless, but they were

hard workers and liked to read. Often homesick, she took out a subscription to *Shufunotomo*, where she read Yamada Waka was going to pay a visit to the United States. Seeing that Seattle was on her intinerary gave her a thrill of anticipation.

"I respected her very much," she told me. "I valued her articles and considered her outlook quite mature. I looked forward to hearing her lecture. Of course, I had no idea that she'd ever been in Seattle before. Then I happened to overhear some customers at our restaurant talking about Yamada. 'That wanton woman,' they said. 'How dare she set foot in this town?' "

Asked what he was referring to, the man sneered, "Ha—that's a good one. The moment she gets on stage, let's make fun of her."

Soon several more Japanese men, mostly in their sixties, were loudly discussing Yamada Waka. They claimed she had once been a harlot on King Street. Some of them were kinder and said, 'Waka was terrific.' They admired her for getting out of the trade and wondered how she had done it. But the majority were prepared to jeer, and snipe they did.

It was a cold blustery winter's day at Japan House Hall at the corner of Washington and Menard when Yamada spoke there. (The Hotel Astor now occupies the site.) Naturally Motoda was anxious to hear her. When she entered the building, the auditorium was already filled to capacity and many were standing in the aisles. The president of the Japan Society gave a short speech, as did some other dignitaries and then Yamada came on stage.

The crowd broke into an uproar. There were shouts of

"Hey, you! Arabian Oyae!" and "Welcome Oyae!" Some swore and cursed at her.

Yamada was conservatively dressed in a plain kimono and wore glasses. It was hard to believe she had been a professional. Once on the stage she stood there quietly, maintained her composure, and did not open her mouth. After a few minutes the audience began to wonder when she would speak. The jeering became less strident, tapered off, then stopped altogether.

In a serious, subdued voice Yamada started to speak in a way that Motoda said she would never forget as long as she lived. "Once I was not worthy of standing before you. But I have been reborn. Because I have been resurrected from hell, I have plenty to tell you."

A hush fell over the auditorium; no one even coughed. Overwhelmed by her sense of dignity, the men in the audience seemed ashamed of their behavior. They remained quiet while she discussed politics, peace, and the role of women. There was not a single interruption.

"I'd heard she was an excellent speaker," Motoda concluded. "But to tell you the truth, I didn't notice. I was much more impressed by the way she handled the jeering audience in her opening remarks. It was the first and only time I met her and I've cherished that memory all these years. She was such a remarkable person. So encouraging. Any unfortunate individual in the audience would have felt it possible to make a fresh start in life."

If Kakichi had still been alive, it is very unlikely he would have permitted Waka to make a public appearance in Seattle. Her willingness to go there suggests she was ready to expose herself to old wounds and did not believe in hiding her past forever. That willingness was also manifested in her visit to Cameron House. Everyone in San Francisco knew what kind of establishment it was and anyone could easily have uncovered Waka's connection with it.

It may be that Waka was not really ashamed of her past. While respecting Kakichi's judgement on the matter, she may not have fully agreed with it. In any event she did not feel she would jeopardize her social status by exposing her past as a prostitute.

Waka's journalistic career was interrupted to some extent after Kakichi's death, although she continued to write for *Shufunotomo*. When war broke out, it figured prominently in Waka's life. The government stressed the importance of human resources and encouraged a higher birthrate with slogans like, "Give birth, more births are needed. Raise healthy children for your country." Waka's views on maternalism went into the war effort. Consequently, when the war ended, Waka might have been viewed as a collaborator and was silenced as a social critic.

If Kakichi had been alive, he would not have allowed her ideas on maternalism to be incorporated into war slogans and propaganda. He despised aggression and Japanese militarism and would not have helped the military clique. But the generous and more naive Waka let herself be used.

Hatagaya School

*O*ne lovely spring day I set out to find the Hatagaya establishments. Obtaining an old map of Shibuya turned out to be rather difficult, and even then I had to ask many people for directions before I reached my destination.

Both the Hatagaya House for Mothers and Children and the Hatagaya Nursery School were leveled to the ground in a fire following an air raid on May 25, 1945. On August 15 of that year, Japan surrendered unconditionally. Shortly after the surrender, Yamada planned to start reconstruction of the center by raising funds in the same manner as she had done previously—by finding volunteers to collect second-hand goods. But those were difficult times. It was a period of widespread scarcity; there were shortages of nearly everything and no one had anything to give away. Yamada requested and received special funding from the welfare ministry. In recognition of her leadership in the movement to protect motherhood, she was presented with half a million yen. She immediately decided to use the funds for a rehabilitation center for women who had a desire to leave the licensed quarters and start a new life.

In prewar Japan, prostitution in licensed houses had been legal. By the end of war the country had more women in this business than at any other time in her history, and with poverty rife throughout the country, the number rose steadily. Nearly every major city had a red light district where a considerable number of women made a living. Then another factor was added: the Allied occupation. According to a booklet bearing the title, "Protecting Women in Metropolitan Tokyo," it seems that one week after Japan's surrender the cabinet held a special meeting on the question of sexual comfort for the officers and men of the occupation. The director general of the police then dispatched the following notice to all district police chiefs throughout the country: "You are urged to take measures that will enable the rapid expansion of sexual comfort facilities, restaurants and bars, and such places of leisure as cafes and dance halls. It is suggested that women for these businesses be recruited mainly from among the geisha, barmaids, waitresses, prostitutes and sexual offenders." The impetus behind this measure was primarily to assure that women from respectable families would be left unmolested by the occupation forces.

In January, 1946, came an abrupt reversal due to a memorandum sent by Allied headquarters to the Japanese government concerning the "abolition of the state regulated prostitution system." It said that the "continuation of licensed prostitution is against democratic ideals" and urged the government to abolish all laws relating to licensed houses. The government complied. All the licensed houses, including the International Friendship Association so recently created by the government, were closed down. But private eating and drinking places were left intact, thus allowing some form of prostitution to continue. Prostitutes discharged from the houses were permitted to operate "on their own initiative." This shift in policy dealt a formidable blow to racketeers, but it also freed many more girls to roam the streets and hover around military bases.

In this climate of licentiousness, poverty and vice, with prostitutes and juvenile offenders becoming the number one social problem, Yamada decided that a rehabilitation school was the most pressing need. The sight of women and girls on street corners waiting to pick up any G.I. disturbed her tremendously, for she, like no one else, had reason to sympathize with them.

Hatagaya Girls School was erected in April, 1947. Other centers of this nature were known as homes, but Yamada called her institution a school, by which she meant that it should be a place where women could learn new skills to help them rebuild their lives.

The 190-square-meter building consisted of five bedrooms, one workroom, an office and a staff room. Waka's sister Hisa became headmistress; her adopted son Tamio was appointed director. Under Waka's watchful eye, they, together with two other staff members, dedicated themselves to guiding the unfortunate women. The school aimed to teach employable skills—dressmaking, knitting, embroidery—anything that would enable a woman to stand on her own feet and earn an honest wage. When a woman reached a certain level of proficiency and emotional stability, she was encouraged to seek outside employment. A woman could remain at the school and commute to and from work.

Obtaining food and equipment was extremely difficult during those postwar days. Potatoes and pumpkins were planted in the school yard and sweet potatoes and rice purchased from a nearby farmer, but in spite of these efforts, the school did not fare well at first. Waka barely managed to keep the women above starvation level. This did nothing to alleviate the already pessimistic, decadent atmosphere. Some women at Hatagaya surrendered to materialistic craving and returned to the streets.

Welfare statistics record that in 1948 ninety-two women were admitted to Hatagaya. Only twenty-seven stuck it out. Of the sixty-five who gave up, twenty-one resumed a normal life (fourteen returned to their homes, one married and six found regular employment). Among the other forty-five, five relocated, one died and thirty-eight ran away. Some in this last group stole school property—sewing machines, knitting instruments—none of which were easy to replace.

Still Waka was not discouraged. She fully understood the attraction of luxury and the minds of those who chose the path of least resistance. Instead of fretting over those who went away, she persevered and worked patiently with the few who chose to remain. In time, the rehabilitation program succeeded.

In 1954 the National Women's Welfare Organization conducted a survey on rehabilitated women. The statistics are revealing. Some case histories of women protected in the centers were written down and documented. Included was the case of a women from Hatagaya to whom the study gave the name Noda Ineko.

Prior to her admission to the Hatagaya Girls School in June, 1949, Noda had lived in Ibaraki Prefecture. Born in 1932 and raised in Tokyo, her childhood was normal until the family was evacuated in 1944 to Ibaraki Prefecture. Difficult times ensued, and tensions in the family heightened. Two of her sisters left home for Tokyo and Noda followed them in May, 1948. She arrived at one of Tokyo's main terminals, Ueno Station, and then wandered around, wondering what to do, where to go. A woman approached her and offered her a place to sleep in return for which Noda was asked to sell bread on the black market. Soon she was forced into prostitution. She was arrested and sent to Rehabilitation Center A, from which she immediately ran away and headed straight back to Ueno Station. She was arrested again, and before long had a string of arrests and a number of short confinements at various centers from which she escaped. She was only sixteen when she was transferred from one center to Hatagaya Girls School. Waka found her to be in good health and above average in intelligence but unstable.

She was taught to make artificial flowers and other skills and was able to get work in a factory. On occasion she still exhibited signs of emotional disturbance. She was stubborn, impudent to teachers and some gave up on her. But a few teachers learned how to handle her and after three years of guidance, a man at the factory proposed marriage. With the school acting as surrogate parents at her wedding in 1952, the bride appeared radiant. After the ceremony, she packed her belongings into a three-wheeled truck and departed. Noda had saved enough from her earnings for a dowry of furniture, pillow cases and some other goods. The newlyweds settled in a village and took out a mortgage on a small house. Both are happy and still working.

It was a victory for Yamada and the Hatagaya Girls School, where she remained until her death from a heart attack in Iga-chō at the age of seventy-eight. The date was September 6, 1956. She had requested a simple funeral and her wishes were respected. According to newspaper stories of her death, many of her old friends from the Seitōsha attended her funeral, among them Hiratsuka, Ichikawa, Yamaoka, Takeuchi, Tokunaga—all fighters for women's causes—as well as some graduates of Hatagaya and several social workers.

In thinking about her work at the school, I realized that Yamada had tried to duplicate her life at Cameron House, where she had been reborn. It was surely that experience that motivated her to choose rehabilitation work as her most important endeavor, her final expression of maternal ideals.

I have said it before but I'll repeat it. Yamada Waka was a winner. And she knew it. She could face a hostile audience, put up with frustration, educate herself at the age of thirty, and virtually undertake anything she wanted to because she was determined, patient and persevering.

In her lifetime she had translated two full-length works into Japanese, wrote for the *Asahi* and composed ten original works. Above all she helped hundreds of women in one way or another. Both in her house and at the Hatagaya School she practiced her belief in maternalism.

The most impressive thing about her remains her character. She had the extraordinary ability to surmount seemingly insurmountable difficulties, although to be sure, she must have wanted to give up often enough. There are those who will say she was lucky. Certainly she was fortunate to have a husband like Yamada Kakichi. But without her constant drive, Waka would never have attained the heights she did. To me and millions of others, Waka will symbolize hope. Her place in Japanese women's history is assured.

定価3,400円
in Japan